TIME SERVED

A Memoir

T.L. Cromwell

KP PUBLISHING COMPANY

TIME SERVED: A Memoir

ISBN: 978-1-960001-19-1 (Hardcover)
ISBN: 978-1-960001-20-7 (Paperback)
ISBN: 978-1-960001-21-4 (Ebook)

Library of Congress Control Number: 2023908331

Editor: Stacie Fugii
Cover Design: Juan Roberts, Creative Lunacy
Literary Director: Sandra Slayton James

Published by:

KP Publishing Company
Publisher of Fiction, Nonfiction & Children's Books
www.kp-pub.com

Printed in the United States of America

CONTENTS

California Institution for Men (CIM)

This book is dedicated to my dear mother.

Thank you for fostering my love of reading.
You sparked the fire that lit my path with your love and guidance.
You are my first love. I will love you until the day I die.
Every day I speak your name.

CHAPTER 1

GROWING UP

When I entered the office, three people were sitting behind a conference table, with a single chair across from them, with a microphone on the table. I was familiar with some of their faces, I'd seen them around the Institution, some not so much. I sat down. I placed my cassette recorder on the table in between us and pressed play.

They read me the Officer's Bill of Rights. I was offered a union representative. I respectfully declined. They asked me why.

"I know my rights and I didn't do anything wrong," I stated. With that, the interview began.

"Officer Cromwell, do you know Officers Reva and Felicity?" He asked.

"Yes," I responded.

"Are you good friends?"

"Yes."

"As good friends, do you tell each other everything?"

"No, of course not, nobody tells anybody everything!"

"Do you know inmate Sylvester?"

"Not personally, but I heard he is an inmate housed in Facility C, in Building 5."

"Have you ever participated in a three-way phone call with the inmate?"

"No."

"If I played you a recording, would you be able to recognize the voices on the tape?"

For the life of me, I didn't understand why they would engage in a telephone conversation with an inmate. We knew all inmate phone calls were recorded.

"No, I wouldn't. How would I know whose voice it is? It could be you pretending to be them."

That was it. The interview was over. I stopped my cassette recorder, picked up my purse, and left the Institution.

The day after the interview, I arrived at work as usual. Unfortunately, for me, nothing would ever be the same again. The first indication that something was wrong was when I stepped into the sally port, which was filled with other staff arriving for work. All conversations stopped. Nobody looked at me. Nobody spoke to me. When the gate opened, everyone stepped aside to let me walk through. In their eyes I was guilty. I continued walking down the roadway to my work assignment. Unfortunately, when I arrived at Central Control the treatment got worse.

* * *

Nobody says they want to work in prison when they grow up. Who would want to be a prison guard? I certainly didn't. I wanted to be what all kids say they want to be when they grow up: a doctor, a lawyer, a social worker, or maybe even a teacher. I had the same dreams and desires as most other kids. If you told me then that I would spend the majority of my adult life in prison, I would have probably laughed in your face—before I cried.

I grew up in the concrete jungle, in the projects of South Central Los Angeles. Unfortunately, as a child, I had relatives who were incarcerated. I didn't know what they were incarcerated for, but I remember how much I enjoyed visiting day. My mother would pile us into our old Chevrolet station wagon, and we would take that long drive to the California Rehabilitation Center (CRC). It was located East of Los Angeles in Norco, California. CRC is a designated rehabilitation prison that houses prisoners convicted of drug crimes. There, the inmates complete a nine-month rehabilitation program. When we would visit, we got in line like the other families. The guards would give us a number and tell us how much time we had to visit. I'd wait impatiently until my relative came out with the other prisoners. He was always dressed in his blue shirt and blue jeans, with his brown shoes polished. He would pick me up and swing me around until I was dizzy. When our visit was over, we'd say our goodbyes, stand in line once again, and go home. The next weekend we'd pile into that old Chevy, and do it all over again, until the day he came home.

I spent the majority of my adult life in prison. It wasn't something I planned to do, but sometimes life can throw you a curveball. I found myself divorced, and raising my daughter alone. I began looking for a career with great pay, benefits, and a retirement plan. I didn't want to struggle the way I watched some women in my family struggle, and I knew I was smart enough that struggling did not have to be my reality.

Every job I had as an adult seemed to lead me to the California Department of Corrections and Rehabilitation (CDCR).

I began what would become my career in law enforcement by working in San Bernardino County Juvenile Hall. The Institution housed both girls and boys from 9 to 17 years old. The kids housed at Juvenile Hall were there for everything from truancy to murder. They were the type of kids who would not listen to their parents and did not respect authority. Juvenile Hall was divided into 12 housing units. The younger kids with minor infractions (like truancy), who were not convicted of a crime, were housed in units 1-3. The kids who were allowed weekend passes were housed in units 4-5. Those kids also had minor infractions and were not convicted of a crime. The kids housed in units 6-10 were convicted of misdemeanors and non-violent felonies. The kids housed in units 11-12 were the worst. They had felony convictions for everything from simple battery to murder. They were mean, angry, and violent and took their anger out on their peers, as well as staff. They were predators. I worked in Juvenile Hall just long enough to know I didn't like working with incarcerated minors. We were limited in what type of discipline we could use, and they needed discipline.

Juvenile Hall was the first time I was racially profiled at work. I was one of two Black women of the four women hired at the same time. I noticed that the other Black woman and I were always assigned to the most dangerous housing units, while the other women were assigned to the lower units with the younger kids. When I noticed the pattern I asked my direct Supervisor, a Hispanic man, why I was only assigned to Housing Units 10–12, which housed the most dangerous kids, his response was, "Cromwell, I know you can handle yourself." He thought that was a compliment. I let him know how racist that was, and that I would like the opportunity to work in the lower units. That taught me a valuable lesson. When you see something unfair, speak up! Never let anyone gaslight you or take advantage of you.

During the time I worked at Juvenile Hall, my family moved from San Bernardino to Fresno, California. I was thankful for an excuse to quit that job. I didn't like the politics and disliked the kids even more. I thought Juvenile Hall was just a stop on my journey to better things.

During the 1980s, the State of California expanded its prison system. It dramatically increased the number of prisons due to the "War on Drugs." As part of this initiative, there was an increase in federal funding for drug control agencies and proposed strict measures, such as mandatory prison sentences for drug crimes. Politicians used "Tough on Crime" as a political slogan to successfully run for office. While judges began sentencing offenders to life and life without parole, prison, and incarceration became a booming business. The State could not build prisons fast enough to house the burgeoning prison population. Simultaneously, California began aggressively recruiting prison guards.

My brother and uncle were the first to join the Department in my family. They joined during a time when there was no Academy training and Correctional Officers reported directly to the prison. You were given basic training before quickly being assigned to your housing unit. They both loved their jobs. My uncle would tell us stories at every family reunion and my brother would suggest I join the Department every chance he got. I refused to listen because I did not want to be a prison guard. I thought I could do better, and secretly, although I thought very highly of my brother and uncle, I did not think highly of the profession.

Instead, I became a Family Support Officer for Fresno County. I loved my job. I loved everything about it. I was proud when I told people what I did for a living.

It never failed that I would become the center of attention at most events and parties. In every crowd, there is always at least one woman receiving child support or should be, and one man that is paying child support, or should be. I was the person they turned to for advice.

As a Family Support Officer, I calculated child support. I also attended court on behalf of the District Attorney to submit the necessary documents for wage garnishment. Our office was a pink ghetto. It consisted primarily of women, and because I was raised in a family of women, I was in my element. I worked there for several years. Unfortunately, because of the county budget, we were repeatedly furloughed. I wasn't sure how I could continue to support myself and my daughter while periodically being laid off. Unemployment was an option during that time, but what I wanted was a stable career.

The next time my brother suggested I join the CDCR, I agreed. It took a full year to complete the process. There were more than ten years between the time my brother and I joined CDCR. During that time, the Department changed quite a bit. The hiring process had become long and arduous. The process included the application, a written test, an oral examination, a physical agility test, and finally a lengthy background check. Additionally, the Department began requiring a six-week Academy in Galt, California, before you could work in a prison. That meant I would have to leave my daughter with my mother during that time.

The State retired the term "prison guard" and replaced it with "Correctional Officer." I liked that. I felt the change described the professional changes, training, and pay scale more accurately. It also commanded more respect. I would later discover that although Correctional Officer was our professional title, when those steel gates closed and the shit hit the fan, we were prison guards. We used both terms interchangeably.

The year it took to complete the process was a long and difficult year. It didn't help that I was unemployed for most of it. I was so sure the Department of Corrections and Rehabilitation was my destiny, that I moved from Fresno to Lancaster to await my Academy date. I lost sleep wondering if I was tough enough for the job or if I was up to the task. I vacillated all year until I was sure the Universe was leading me in the right direction. Then I received the letter that changed my life.

CHAPTER 2

THE FIRST DAY OF THE REST OF MY LIFE

On July 16, 1994, I arrived at the Galt Correctional Academy with mixed emotions. I was optimistic, but I was also nervous. I didn't know what to expect and I didn't like the unknown. I had prepared myself as much as possible, but I would be lying if I didn't admit I was still scared. I needed a new career that paid well and had good benefits so I could take care of my family, and I had chosen this one.

The only training facility for the California Department of Corrections and Rehabilitation, is the Richard A. McGee Correctional Training Center, which is located on Twin Cities Road in Galt, California. The grounds originally housed the St. Pius Catholic School and had plenty of room for the training and housing of Correctional Officer candidates.

Correctional Officers must complete a six-week formal, comprehensive training program at the Basic Correctional Officer Academy (BCOA). Cadets attend classes five days a week and must pass all classes/tests to graduate. The curriculum consists of 240 hours of training and is one of the country's top three Correctional Training Academies. The training was a two-week course when the facility opened in 1983. Over time, the program expanded to six weeks, then thirteen weeks. Cadets get reality-based training so they can experience as close to real-life situations as possible.

If you told me when I was in school studying to be a social worker, that ultimately, I would be a prison guard, I wouldn't have believed you. I remember reading an article once that referred to prison guards as "knuckle-dragging neanderthals," and I agreed with that description, even though I had family that worked as prison guards. I thought I was too smart and destined to be something else. I always thought I would have a career helping people. Who could I possibly help as a prison guard? At that time, the California Department of Corrections was the furthest career option from my mind.

So, when I arrived at the Academy I was a fish out of water. I was out of my element. I was never an athlete. I didn't like working out, and don't get me started on my disdain for sweating. I was a proud "smart girl" and that had always worked for me. Now my physical endurance would be just as necessary as my intelligence—and that scared me the most.

On the first day, I checked in at the front desk, and was directed to the Academy auditorium. I wanted to get there a little early, as I never liked being late, and wanted to get the lay of the land. When I walked into the auditorium several hundred people were already there. I guess I had the right idea, but from the look of things, I wasn't the only one who had it.

We hung around for about an hour, getting acclimated to our surroundings and sizing each other up. Finally, the program started. We were given a hearty welcome by the Academy Director, then given the rules, regulations, and expectations. These tenets would control and shape our lives for the rest of our careers. After the welcome program, our names were called. They gave us our brown and tan uniforms. Correctional cadets are not allowed to wear the Correctional Officer uniform until graduation day. We received our rooms and were introduced to our roommates. I was assigned two other young ladies. We were given a four-person room, with two bunk beds. We were alphabetically assigned to our companies. Since my last name began with a C, I was assigned to Bravo Company.

Each company was assigned a Guest Company Commander (GCC), as well as a Junior Company Commander (JCC), a cadet who volunteered for the position. The JCC position came with additional responsibilities, in addition to the requirements of a cadet. You know that old Army saying, "Never volunteer for anything?" Well, I usually followed that advice. For some reason, I failed to do so at the Academy. I didn't volunteer for JCC, because I thought it had too many additional responsibilities and I was there trying to get in and out as easily as possible. For some reason, don't ask me why, I volunteered to be the flag-bearer for Bravo Company. A flag-bearer is a person that leads the formal procession; that person marches in front of the company while carrying the giant company flag. Yea, that was a great position for a girl with zero upper body strength, and until I got used to the flag's weight, it was a real struggle. Now, I don't know if it was because somewhere in the back of my mind, I always regretted not being a cheerleader in high school or what, but until this day, I can't for the life of me understand why I volunteered. There was no glory, just extra work.

In CDCR, an assignment to the Academy was considered prestigious. Our GCC was a Correctional Sergeant who was assigned to the Academy from a surrounding Institution. She was tall and statuesque. She was a Black woman with 20-plus years of service in CDCR. She wore the hell out of that uniform. The smoky hat she wore daily was tilted slightly over the top of her eyes. She spoke and carried herself with such confidence, it made you stop and stare. I don't remember her name but she made a lasting impression on me. I wanted to be just like her when I grew up!

Our JCC was a rather smallish cadet from Northern California. What he lacked in size he made up for in spirit. He was kind, helpful, and very motivational. He helped me several times throughout the most difficult six weeks of my life!

He was always pushing me, even when I originally couldn't run that mile in less than 15 minutes. Always championing my efforts. I'm glad he volunteered for the job.

I met my two roommates and we were released to our room assignments. Only to return to that very location the next morning to start our new adventure. The Department of Corrections and Rehabilitation is a paramilitary organization, so it didn't surprise me that it was set up like the barracks of a military base or a college dormitory. The room had two double bunks, a small bathroom, and an even smaller dressing area. Somehow, I drew the short straw and had an upper bunk. I had not slept in a bunk bed since I was a kid. Thank goodness I was still in my twenties because if I was any older, like quite a few of my fellow cadets, it would have been a problem. The oldest cadet in our class was in his sixties, as the Department doesn't have an official maximum age limit. I thought he would have a tough go. I just hoped he would make it through. For many cadets who were not ex-military or who never lived in college dormitories, this was a new experience.

Learning to live in close quarters with people who are not related to you takes some getting used to. Some acclimated faster than others. A few couldn't handle it, but a few room changes seemed to settle the problem.

There were open dormitories that housed the male cadets. The rooms for two, three, or four people were reserved for female cadets, as we were greatly outnumbered. There were six females in Bravo Company, and only two of us were assigned to the same prison. Of course, after the first day, we sought each other out. It made it easier to make friends and help each other make it through the Academy. It felt good to know we would already know someone when we arrived at our assigned Institution.

There are three parts to the Basic Correctional Officer Academy:

1. Academics – we had required classroom time each day, five days a week.
2. Physical Fitness/Agility – we did calisthenics, aerobics, and weight training each morning. We were required to pass the timed mile, sit-ups, push-ups, and obstacle course to successfully pass the Academy.
3. The Shooting Range – The range included the baton, pepper spray, and qualification on all three departmental weapons: the .38 Smith and Wesson, the shotgun, and the Heckler & Koch (H&K) assault rifle.

Academics – We were given a syllabus on the second day of the Academy. It included U.S. History, The U.S. Constitution, as well as a myriad of other subjects. We were required to pass each subject with a minimum score of 70% or we would be on academic probation. Those cadets who found themselves on academic probation would be denied weekend liberty and given extra duties to perform. Of course, the academic portion was my favorite part and came relatively easy to me. I always did well in school. If you graduated from high school there was no reason to believe you could not pass the academic portion of the Academy.

Physical Fitness/Agility – This portion of the Academy was difficult for me, as I was not by any stretch of the imagination physically fit. I had a love/hate relationship with exercise. I didn't particularly like being outside or the weather, and yet here I was, and my new career depended on me overcoming my disdain for exercise, as well as all things physical.

When I arrived at the Academy, I could barely run a complete mile and would have only done so if I was being chased. I would be out of breath and could not complete the entire mile without stopping. As I found myself huffing and puffing around that ¼ mile track, I kept my eyes on the prize.

Pictures of my daughter and the life we could have played over and over in my head until my burning lungs and screaming joints would take a backseat to my future. No more living paycheck to paycheck. I would be able to buy us a house. I would be able to send my daughter to college. We could take annual vacations without having to rob Peter to pay Paul. As a divorced mother, the struggle was real. I knew the older she got, the more she would need. I was willing to do everything in my power to meet her needs. Even if it meant wearing a uniform, boots, and walking the toughest beat in the state. Gratefully, I could already do the required sit-ups during the allotted timeframe. Unfortunately, I had never done a complete push-up in my entire life. I remember not being able to make the President's physical fitness list in middle school because I couldn't do one traditional push-up. That never changed. It was a good thing we were allowed to do the female version of push-ups on our knees with our ankles crossed, or I know I would have failed the Academy.

The Shooting Range – It turned out to be the bane of my existence and it would take everything in me to master it. I swore the range would not be my demise.

Much like the military, before long days of studying, we were also required to keep our assigned rooms and dormitory bunk areas clean and ready for inspection at any time. There were inmate workers at the Academy, brought in daily from a surrounding Institution, but for the most part, we were the underpaid labor force. We were paid an hourly wage that amounted to slightly above minimum wage, during our time in the Academy until we graduated and reported to our assigned Institution.

Due to the pay scale, the Academy was a hardship for some and an investment for others. If you were the head of a household, a single parent, or had a spouse that did not work, it could be a financial hardship and hard to make ends meet. We were also required to purchase our toiletries, as well as our uniforms upon graduation. I met a few cadets who moved back in with their parents, and some who refinanced their homes or took out loans given that they knew being a Correctional Officer was an investment in their future.

It didn't take two days before the entire Academy class was in trouble. It was thought that some knucklehead brought his weapon on grounds, because live ammunition was found in the trashcans and turned into the front desk. This was a problem because of the presence of inmates from the surrounding Institutions who worked as Academy porters and clerks. It was their job to empty the trashcans. Imagine live ammunition being taken inside an Institution by an inmate. Just imagine. Fortunately, the inmate who found it turned it in, and because of that incident, we were denied our first weekend liberty. That stunt was just a harbinger of things to come.

Rumors circulated that there was talk of firing the entire class, if nobody came forward. I couldn't believe my future was hanging on some moron who thought it was a good idea to bring a weapon with live ammunition to the Academy. Nobody ever came forward. Thank God that rumor turned out to be just that, a rumor.

I quickly realized that everything at the Academy was a competition. Everybody was competing against each other. Each company competes against the other, and the men compete against the women. Who could do the most push-ups, sit-ups, and run the fastest mile? Who was the best academically, as well as who was the best marksman at the shooting range? I don't know why I thought it would be more of a collective, where we all worked together to help each other get through.

The men dominated the physical competitions, as well as the range, and the women dominated academically. Occasionally, we would kick their butts in something physical. It was usually something inconsequential that you would never win a prize for. Step aerobics became one of those things. Like most women, I had taken step aerobics classes for years. What woman didn't have a Jane Fonda or Richard Simmons CD hiding in a drawer in their house somewhere? So, when morning aerobics was added to the syllabus, we were ecstatic. It beat the hell out of running around the track every morning. Little did we know it would be a disaster for the men. During the class, some uncoordinated men would become disoriented. Some would miss a step, trip, and fall. I think a few even passed out. It shouldn't have been funny. Oh, but it was. We enjoyed it immensely! It didn't mean anything in the long run, but it was great for our morale.

We were given weekends off beginning Friday night. Having to report back at 8:00 a.m. Monday morning. It was a godsend for many. Especially for the cadets that lived in Northern California because they could easily go home for the weekend and report back on Monday. For the rest of us from Southern California and other parts of the United States, it was not as simple. Most of us could not afford last-minute airfare, as our pay was so low, and it was too far to drive with the possibility of not arriving back in time on Monday morning. So usually, we stayed at the Academy during those weekends, sleeping there at night but leaving during the day to explore the surrounding areas.

If you slept at the Academy each night during the weekend the curfew was 2:00 a.m. and you were required to check in and out at the front desk. Unfortunately, many cadets did not respect themselves, the Academy, or their fellow cadets enough to behave appropriately. There were always drunken cadets staggering back in after curfew. It was ridiculous! I did not like it one bit. These were the people who would take the oath and swear to uphold the law and they were behaving like immature frat boys or sorority girls! Depending on how inappropriate the behavior was, liberty could be canceled for the rest of the weekend for the remaining cadets on the grounds due to no fault of our own. I can't tell you how many times drunken cadets were laughing and carrying on in the halls, giggling, falling, throwing up, and generally disturbing the peace until liberty was canceled altogether. The women were the absolute worst! They would dress inappropriately, behave inappropriately, and do things that they should be ashamed of. If their repeated actions were any indication, they weren't. They treated the Academy like a hall pass from their husbands and their home life. What happens at the Academy stays at the Academy became the unspoken motto.

When the drunken women would stagger in, half-dressed, inevitably all female cadets would have a mandatory meeting and would be dressed down about any number of topics; inappropriate behavior, dressing inappropriately, fraternizing with other cadets as well as Academy staff. It was always the same offenders, week after week until liberty was canceled altogether, just for the women. If we weren't afraid of being kicked out of the Academy we would have handled it old school style, but we couldn't. Imagine being sent home only to have to explain to your husband, or family, you were kicked out for fighting. I was furious. We couldn't do anything about it, but talk amongst ourselves, silently seethe and give the offenders the silent treatment. I didn't understand why we were being punished for the actions of a few. Why not discipline the offender or better yet kick them out of the Academy? What type of Officers would they make anyway? We did our best to avoid them and concentrated instead on passing the Academy. If they behaved like that during the strict confines of the Academy, I shuddered to think how they would behave at the Institution.

There was so much sex going on at the Academy that frankly, it made my head spin. Of course, it was against the Academy's policy and generally frowned upon; however, they were consenting adults, so what could they do about it? I guess when you put men and women in tight quarters, away from home, things like that happen. There were rumors about multiple hookups with single as well as married cadets. I wondered how many cadets on the brink of failure passed the Academy because of such shenanigans.

Of course, there were always rumors. Who could be sure? Frankly, I didn't know how those people found the time. I'm no prude by any means. I was in my 20s and away from home too. I knew how to have a good time, but there was a time and place for such foolishness, and this was not it.

When I went to the Academy, I had to leave my daughter with my mother for the summer. She was nine years old at the time. It was the first time in her life that I was away that long. I took my responsibilities very seriously. Graduation could not come fast enough!

CHAPTER 3

EYES ON THE PRIZE

During the second week of the Academy, we began going to the shooting range. One of the requirements to graduate was to qualify with the three departmental weapons:

1. The .38 Smith & Wesson – which was for personal protection.
2. The Shotgun – for crowd control.
3. The H&K – for everything else.

Before applying to the Department, I had rarely touched a gun. I was staunchly against them, but because I understood weapons qualification would be one of my responsibilities, I went to the local shooting range to familiarize myself with guns before my arrival.

I am not a pacifist, but I truly believe that gun violence and the proliferation of guns cause too many avoidable problems in society. Although mass shootings had not yet become the norm, too many people were killed or incarcerated due to the accessibility of guns, both legal and illegal. Now, I was required to understand the nomenclature, be able to disassemble, clean, re-assemble, and qualify with three different weapons to graduate from the Academy.

I was very confident that qualifying with firearms would not be a problem for me. Imagine my surprise when I failed to do so. I failed to qualify with the .38 Smith & Wesson. I was devastated. Since we typically went to the range on Mondays, I had the entire week to brood and be out of sorts. It threw me off my game. As a result, my academic performance suffered. Unfortunately, I am a perfectionist. I could be great at everything, except one thing. That one thing would be the only thing I could concentrate on and it would throw me off in everything else. I attempted to qualify three times. I failed every time, and I was placed in remedial training. At that point, I wasn't even sure I would pass the Academy and graduate. I panicked.

Each time I failed the range I stayed on grounds over the weekend when the other cadets would leave on liberty. I took remedial training each weekend, and each time I failed. The interesting part is my instructors couldn't seem to identify my problem. I had my theory. I was left-handed. All my life I have had problems because of it. So, when I shot the weapon, I usually veered off my target to the left. There were several times I shot on the target of the cadet standing to the left of me. He would have more holes than bullets. I always knew I was the culprit, although I didn't say anything. Whatever my problem was I was absolutely at the end of my rope. I had one last time to attempt to qualify before I would fail the Academy, and be recycled. If you failed the Academy, you are allowed to go to the next scheduled Academy to start all over again, and you are assigned to a new company.

Each Academy was six weeks long. If I was recycled, I'd have to stay for 12 weeks. I couldn't be away from my kid that long and it would be financially devastating.

Then, if I failed the re-cycled Academy I would be dismissed and would have to wait a year to start the process all over again. Failure was not an option for me.

I decided to leave the Academy one weekend. I went to Fresno to my mom's house to take my mind off my failure, to have her pray for me, and see my kid. I hadn't seen her in weeks and maybe she'd be the motivation I needed to do what I needed to do. While there, I also went to a local range and concentrated on my shooting. The range owner gave me some great tips. He said my problem was I veered off to the left because I wasn't breathing correctly, and I wasn't appropriately utilizing my front and rear sights. He gave me a few pointers and wished me well.

When I returned to the Academy on Monday morning, I couldn't wait to get to the range. I was ready. This was my last shot. This time would be for all the marbles.

When we got to the range, we were handed our holsters, our speed loaders, our weapons, and our rounds. I secured my left-handed holster to my strong side, placed my speed loader on my belt, and all my rounds in my weak side pocket.

Our first course of fire would be from the three-yard line. When we lined up in front of our targets, I just happened to be standing next to the best shooter at the Academy. He always shot a perfect score, 36 out of 36. Unfortunately for him, he was standing to my left. I quickly leaned over and told him my dilemma that I ALWAYS shot to my left and there was a good chance I would shoot his target. I advised him to drop a round or he'd probably be disqualified. More than 36 holes in your target would get you disqualified. I didn't think that was fair, but that was the rule.

I was as ready as I would ever be. The Range Master began yelling instructions!

"Cadets, this first course of fire will be shooting from your hip from the three-yard line. Load your speed loader with six rounds and place six rounds in your weapon. Then holster your weapon!" He instructed anyone with any issues to raise their hand. When nobody raised their hand, he continued.

"Ready on the right? Ready on the left? Cadets begin shooting!"

I un-holstered my weapon. Pushed it out in front of me. Placed my finger on the trigger. Took a deep breath. And began shooting. When I was done, I holstered my weapon. One of the best things about shooting from the three-yard line is you can see where all your rounds landed on your target. It gave me a big boost of confidence when I quickly counted all twelve rounds at center mass.

We were instructed to turn around and walk back to the seven-yard line. Again, we placed six rounds in our speed loader; six rounds in our weapons. Then holstered our weapon. Again, the Range Master began yelling instructions:

"Cadets, this course of fire will be instinctive shooting from the seven-yard line." He asked anyone with any issues to raise their hand. When nobody raised their hand, he continued.

"Ready on the right? Ready on the left? Cadets begin shooting!"

I un-holstered my weapon. Utilized my front and rear sights. Placed my finger on the trigger. Took a deep breath and slowly released it as I began shooting. When we finished that course of fire, we walked back to the fifteen-yard line. The exact scenario played out once again. When we were done shooting, we were instructed to police our brass as we slowly walked down to the three-yard line to await our fate.

As I got closer and closer to my target, I began counting the holes. By the time I reached the three-yard line the range assistant had just finished writing my score in the upper left-hand corner. I could see my score from where I was standing.

My final score was 34 out of 36. I had done it. I qualified. I was ecstatic, almost giddy. A huge weight was lifted off my shoulders. When we were cleared to approach our targets, I counted the holes. I only had 35 holes; one round was missing. The cadet to the left of me winked at me, as once again he shot a perfect score. My mother's prayers were answered and the weapons qualification was not my demise.

CHEMICAL AGENTS

After what felt like an eternity, we finally made it to the last week of the Academy. Our last class was instruction on the Department's two chemical agents:

> **Oleoresin Capsicum** (OC) – The oil comes from plants in the genus capsicum, which includes chili peppers. It is utilized for self-defense and crowd control.
>
> **Chlorobenzalmalononitrile** (CS) – It is a chemical compound that is used for crowd and riot control.

We learned when it is appropriate to deploy each chemical agent and the effects on the population we were attempting to control. We were each assigned a gas mask. It was very important to learn how to appropriately seal the mask, as well as how to clean it. If you didn't get a good seal, you would quickly regret it and suffer the consequences.

On the last day, we donned our gas masks and walked through the gas chamber, which was a modified shipping container. One instructor stood at the opening, one was inside, and one was stationed at the end. The instructors were there to keep us from becoming disoriented while inside the chamber. The container was filled with copious amounts of oleoresin capsicum. We walked in one by one.

When I entered the chamber, my mask immediately began filling with chemical agents. The chemicals burned my eyes and nose. At the halfway point everyone was required to remove their masks and recite their name, company, and social security number. By the time I was on the other side, all I could do was thank God and gulp as much air as possible to clear my lungs. The gas chamber separated the men from the boys, as the pepper spray had negative effects on several cadets. I made it through my last rite of passage before graduation.

ON THE JOB TRAINING

During the six-week Academy, we were required to complete on-the-job training (OJT) at one of the surrounding prisons. The assigned location was based on your company. Bravo Company was assigned to Deuel Vocational Institution (DVI). I had heard many horror stories about OJT. It wasn't unusual for cadets to return from OJT and drop out of the Academy altogether. There was always one or two in each Academy class. OJT was the first glimpse a cadet had into the culture and daily workings of a real prison. This was our first real contact with inmates, and without protection. The training wheels were coming off. We were required to work a full shift with a seasoned prison guard in some of the most violent housing units in the State. We were assigned partners and the expectation was we would arrive together and leave the same way we came. In other words, we were responsible for each other. My partner and I were assigned to the Level II housing unit.

DEUEL VOCATION INSTITUTION (DVI)

Deuel Vocational Institution is a state prison located in the unincorporated San Joaquin County near Tracy, California. It was opened in 1953 and has a population of around 2,000 male inmates. One purpose of DVI is to serve as a Reception Center for newly committed prisoners to CDCR from Northern California county jails. It also houses "mainline" inmates classified as Level I and Level II. Additionally, there is a minimum security "ranch" that supports a dairy. As a result of DVI's primary function as a Reception Center, many convicted felons of different propensities for violence, disciplinary and security issues passed through before being classified and transferred to other facilities. DVI has a long-standing reputation for being violent and dangerous. The Institution used to be referred to as "gladiator school" by inmates and staff because DVI was widely known for fights and homicides that took place within the prison walls. Its claim to fame is that the Mexican Mafia was established there.

We were assigned to a general population housing unit and for good or bad we were partnered with an old prison guard, who had worked there for 23 years. Our Academy uniforms were tan and brown. It resembled the uniform of a UPS delivery person. Remember, we were not allowed to wear the tan/green Correctional Officer uniform until we graduated from the Academy, therefore, we stuck out like a sore thumb. The inmates could easily identify us. They could smell our fear. They knew we were inexperienced, which inevitably made us a target. I was happy when the Department changed that policy, retired the UPS uniform, and assigned the cadets the Correctional Officer tan/green uniform on the very first day.

We survived the day in that old unit with that old prison guard. For the most part, it was a pleasant experience. We released the inmates for chow, then locked them back up. We released them for dayroom, then locked them back up again. Unfortunately, because it was an old Institution I could not open the cell doors electronically, like all the newer 180 and 270 design Institutions. We were required to use the antiquated Folger Adams keys that CDCR has used since its inception, and it was hard on our hands. I couldn't imagine doing that every day for 25 years. We ran the programs, phones, and released the inmates to the yard, school, and work. The only experience I could have done without is that the old guard continuously regaled us with the stories of his life and career, which included many tales of him being assaulted. He even showed us his scars and "war" wounds. Such stories and actions could scare and scar a new cadet, which may have been the point. At DVI, the old guard had to walk down the tiers to unlock each cell manually. When it was time for dayroom release, the Officer stationed me and my fellow cadet at the beginning of each tier, closest to the door as he went down the tier opening each cell door. As he opened each cell, the inmates would step out. It looked like the Officer was being swallowed up by inmates as he continued down the tier, away from us, and away from the exit. After release, he was down at the other end of the tier, with the inmates between him and us.

Even though we were stationed closest to the exit he had the only key to the door with him at the back of the tier. You talk about terrified! That was my first lesson in "Never let them see you sweat." That lesson would serve me well throughout my career. When I asked him why he released that way, instead of going to the end of the tier and walking toward the exit as he released the building, he said, he always did it that way and would continue to do so. He was a dinosaur—unable or unwilling to learn anything new, even if his life depended on it.

I felt like I was living through an episode of Scared Straight! You know that TV show where wayward teenagers are taken to prison to deter them from their criminal behavior?

I didn't know what to think about the experience. I knew Los Angeles County (LAC) was a new Institution. It was a 270 designed prison. The design was to alleviate blind spots that plagued the older Institutions. The cells were electronically controlled, the Folger Adam keys were no longer used to open and close each cell. It wasn't built like DVI. I had a lot to think about on our trip back to the Academy. What I already knew for sure was that I wouldn't be one of those girls who quit after OJT. I still had way more to gain than I had to lose.

When we got back to the Academy, I heard several female cadets quit. The stress of the Institution was too much for them. Not me! I was on to graduation and a brand new career.

GRADUATION DAY

Graduation day finally arrived. I had completed my assignments, passed all my classes and qualified with the weapons. I was ready to graduate. The day before, I purchased my Correctional Officer uniform and shined my boots. I was raring to go. That morning we assembled in front of the Academy to march to the auditorium where we were greeted by our family and friends. I was blessed to have my baby girl in attendance. It was one of the proudest moments of my life, as she watched me get my badge pinned to my shirt. It was wonderful to see people from every race, color, and gender. As Bravo Company's flag-bearer, I was out front leading the parade along with the other flag-bearer of each company.

It was interesting to see the most problematic cadets with their spouses and families. Especially, the ones who had engaged in relationships while there. They were the ones who had their spouses pin their badges to their shirts. One of the Academy's biggest playboys, who engaged in all sorts of nefarious activities while there was pinned by his fiancée. We were shocked to learn he was engaged.

Unfortunately, he was also headed to LAC. His fiancée was a Correctional Counselor who worked there. I was disheartened to see her pride and adoration while pinning his badge to his chest. From then on, every time I saw him, all I could see were his actions at the Academy. We would nod and continue along our way. We kept to the unwritten rule we established at the Academy, "What happens at the Academy, stays at the Academy!" His secret was safe with me.

Once we assembled in the auditorium, the administrators and dignitaries led us through our graduation ceremony. The introduction included each company's achievements, and any cadet in the company that earned top honors in academics, physical fitness, and the shooting range. I did not earn anything, except my ticket to a better life, and that was enough for me.

Speeches were given, hands were shaken, and babies were kissed; all the pomp and circumstance required for a graduation ceremony. We were called on stage, given our graduation certificates, and pinned with our badges. Each cadet was allowed to have a person of their choosing pin their badge to their shirts. It was heartwarming to see mothers and fathers, spouses, and sometimes even adult children pin the badge to the shirt of their cadet. It was one of the proudest moments of my life. The code of ethics was read. We stood, raised our right hand, and repeated after the CDCR director who administered our oath:

THE PEACE OFFICERS OATH

"I, T.L. Cromwell, do solemnly swear or affirm that I will support and defend the Constitution of the United States and the Constitution of the State of California against all enemies, foreign and domestic; that I will bear true faith and allegiance to the Constitution of the United States and the Constitution of the State of California that I take this obligation freely, without any mental reservation or purpose of evasion; and that I will well and faithfully discharge the duties upon which I am about to enter.

And I do further swear or affirm that I do not advocate, nor am I a member of any party or organization, political or otherwise, that now advocates the overthrow of the Government of the United States or of the State of California by force or violence or other unlawful means; that within the five years immediately preceding the taking of the oath or affirmation I have not been a member of any party or organization, political or otherwise, that advocated the overthrow of the Government of the United States or of the State of California by force or violence or other unlawful means except as follows; I will not advocate nor become a member of any party or organization, political or otherwise, that advocates the overthrow of the Government of the United States or of the State of California by force or violence or other unlawful means."

After the ceremony, we were welcomed into the CDCR family. I scooped up my daughter. I packed my things, and threw them in the back of my car. I burnt rubber getting the hell out of dodge! I was driving down Highway 99 within the hour. I felt so good.

I rolled down the window to feel the warmth of the summer breeze on my face, while I blasted "Lay Your Troubles Down" by Angela Winbush on the radio. The lyrics in that song resonated with me. After the six weeks I just experienced, I felt it in my soul! We sang along.

By the time I looked up, I could see the skyline of Fresno in the distance. I stopped just long enough to share my accomplishment with my family. It was a beautiful day as we hopped back on Highway 99. We began singing the song in unison, in earnest, as we drove South into our future.

I left the Basic Correctional Officer Academy (BCOA) that day excited about the next chapter of my life. I was scheduled to start work the following Monday at the California State Prison – Los Angeles County (CSP-LAC).

CALIFORNIA STATE PRISON LOS ANGELES COUNTY (CSP-LAC)

CHAPTER 4

LAC: INTRODUCTION TO PRISON

California State Prison – Los Angeles County (CSP-LAC) is a male-only state prison located in the City of Lancaster, in Los Angeles County, California. It is the only state prison located in the county.

When the Department was determining where the first state prison in Los Angeles County was to be built, the director encountered multiple roadblocks. Sometimes, it was difficult to convince civic and city leaders that a state prison would be a positive addition to its community. The fear was it would bring inmate families into the city which would cause increased crime. When the inmate population was paroled from the prison, instead of moving back to wherever they were living when they were apprehended, they would remain in the city with their families. Unfortunately, sometimes those fears proved true.

Within its first year of operation, LAC earned the dubious distinction of being the only state prison to have four escapes. The community was up in arms and outraged. As a result, the Warden retired, and several staff were disciplined as well. Due to the escapes, LAC installed an electrified fence to ensure maximum-security inmates would never escape again. Unfortunately, the same cannot be said for minimum-security inmates. In 2017, Inmate Jason Kohr walked away from the minimum support facility. He was later apprehended in Mountain View, California.

LAC employs over 1,200 staff. It has a design capacity of 2,200 inmates, but had a population of over 4,200. The prison was operating well over its designed capacity. LAC's 262 acres included: Level I Housing; open dormitories without a secure perimeter, which means it doesn't have a guard tower, but is surrounded by barbed wire; Level III and Level IV Housing; cells and fenced or walled perimeters, electric fencing, and more staff and armed Officers both inside and outside the Institution. The Reception Center (RC), provides short-term housing to process, classify and evaluate incoming inmates. LAC also has a Sensitive Needs Yard (SNY), which houses inmates who have agreed to refrain from prison politics and drop out of gang activities. Additionally, it houses inmates who are particularly vulnerable to sexual and physical exploitation due to their age and/or sexual orientation.

LAC is located in the Northernmost reaches of Los Angeles County in the Antelope Valley. Since it is still in Los Angeles County, the majority of the inmate population is from Los Angeles and surrounding vicinities. The bright lights of the city, unfortunately, belong to a Level IV men's prison.

Before the prison opened in 1993, Los Angeles County had no prisons but accounted for 40% of California's state prison population. The Institution was affectionately nicknamed "Chocolate City" due to the large number of Black inmates as well as correctional staff.

On August 29, 1994, I arrived at CSP-LAC having graduated from the Academy the Friday before. I was one of two Black women that reported. After I graduated from the Academy, I was required to report to my designated Institution on the following Monday for a week of OJT. As a cadet, I remember that old prison guard at DVI telling us, "The Academy is where you are trained how to be a Correctional Officer, but the prison is where you learn how to do your job!" I was looking forward to it.

As usual, I made sure I arrived early to hopefully get the lay of the land. Although I was apprehensive and afraid, you couldn't tell by my demeanor. That is where my "fake 'til you make it" mantra began. It would serve me well throughout my career. I was relieved to have a week to catch my breath and get my bearings before I was thrown from the frying pan into the fire. Over the next week, I met the Warden as well as other administrative staff. We toured each facility and became acclimated to prison life. The administrative staff was comprised of a good percentage of women, many of them Black. It was wonderful to see female Sergeants, Lieutenants, and Associate Wardens. When I looked around, I saw my potential career path mapped out for me.

The week of OJT consisted of: use of force, mental health, a Warden's forum, and the shooting range on the final day. During range, I was ecstatic that weapons qualification was no longer an issue and could finally fade into the background. From then on, the annual range visit would become something I looked forward to. During the first week, we had little to no inmate contact. The only contact we had was with the inmate workers, consisting mostly of clerks, porters, and cooks that worked in the administration building. When we toured the facilities, we were still relatively protected by our instructors and seasoned staff.

Before I had any personal experience inside prisons, I thought prisoners were mostly unlucky people who had made bad choices and decisions. Eventually, I found out how wrong I was. Of course, some inmates kept to themselves and just did their time. The majority of them, however, I would discover had a criminal mentality. Most of them were predators. I wasn't sure if they arrived that way or if they simply adapted to the prison environment. What I did know is, they had 365 days to scheme and scam everyone who crossed their paths, especially their families. So many of the inmates were smart and talented. I always wondered where some of them would be if they had chosen a different path. What if they had used their gifts for good, instead of evil? For some of the inmates, what if they had not been born into their families, or lived in their neighborhoods, would they be different? Who knows? I didn't have long to concentrate on such things because it was the end of OJT and I would report to my first assignment on Monday.

On Sunday night I received a phone call, which I was simultaneously looking forward to, and dreading at the same time. It was from the Watch Office offering me my first assignment. I had no choice but to accept the assignment because I was a Permanent Intermittent Employee, PIE for short. A PIE is an employee who did not have a full-time, permanent position and was hired to work a certain number of hours annually. PIEs were also on call and could not refuse an assignment. I accepted a PIE assignment because it was the only way to work at LAC. I accepted every position they called me for. Eventually, I learned how to work my status to my benefit. If I wanted to ensure I worked on a particular yard, I called in early and requested it. If I didn't want to work that day I simply wouldn't answer my phone. My very first assignment was Facility D, Housing Unit 2, Control Booth Officer.

As expected, I didn't get much sleep that night. I was restless. I was nervous because I didn't know what to expect the next day. All night I was praying I wouldn't have to shoot someone. The next morning, I got up early, and put on my brand-new uniform and my freshly shined boots.

I packed my lunch in my new lunch cooler and was off to my first day in prison. I arrived early for my assignment. I wanted to be a good relief and give the Officer I was relieving at least 30 minutes to explain everything to me. Unfortunately, it didn't work out quite as I anticipated. He must have seen me coming. The Control Booth Officer saw my eagerness as an opportunity to leave thirty minutes early. He grabbed his things and rushed out of the Control Booth so fast that when he popped the button and entered the sally port, he neglected to show me how to pop him out of the housing unit. He had to explain it to me through the portal in the ceiling. As soon as he explained it, and I popped the button and opened the sally port door, he was gone.

Thank goodness for post orders. They were my saving grace. There are post orders for every position in prison, and the post orders explain the Officer's responsibilities for their shift. Once I read them, I understood the assignment and the expectations for the post.

Each housing unit had three Officers assigned to the building. There is a strict Officer to inmate ratio, negotiated by the Peace Officer Union, which had to be followed. There are two Floor Officers, and one Control Booth Officer per building. The Control Booth Officer is in control of the housing unit. The Control Booth Officer's primary responsibility is equipment accountability. All housing unit equipment is housed in the Control Booth, which is a secured location away from the inmate population. Additionally, the Control Booth Officer is responsible for all doors, all areas of ingress, and egress. The opening and closing of all cell doors, releasing the housing unit for all activities for that shift; showers, recreational yard, chow, education, work, vocation, medical, disciplinary hearings, groups, all appointments, and visiting. Inmates can't make a move without the Control Booth Officer allowing it. Over the years the Control Booth Officer became my preferred assignment because I liked having very little direct contact with inmates.

After I thoroughly read and signed my post orders, I completed the equipment check, familiarized myself with the control panel, strapped my .38 pistol to my hip, slung my H&K across my back, and started my first shift.

The day ran smoothly. I prepared my building for morning chow release, released the inmates to the chow hall, and then locked them back up upon their return. I released the inmate population to their various daily assignments. Then finally, released the dayroom and recreational yard. At that time of the day, there is the least number of inmates in the building. Usually, just a handful who preferred the dayroom to the yard, or those who stayed back to make their daily telephone calls. The Control Booth Officer also had control of the building phones. You are required to randomly listen to phone calls. You could disconnect the call if something sounded unusual or strange. The inmates were barred from three-way, and threatening phone calls. I developed a reputation for disconnecting telephone contact if an inmate became the least bit disrespectful, threatening, or harassed the person on the other end of the line. Of course, that did not make me very popular with the inmates, and I didn't care. Protecting the public from the inmate population was part of my duties, and I took it very seriously.

There were two Floor Officers assigned to each building, and D2 was no different. Each Floor Officer position had its post orders and required duties. Each Floor Officer was required to complete three cell searches per shift, per day. The purpose was to keep the cells clean of contraband and unnecessary debris. You could easily tell which Officers, in which housing units did not do their required cell searches, based on the appearance of the cells in particular, and the housing unit, in general.

Since it was the slowest part of the day, with the least number of inmates in the housing unit, the Officers began their required searches.

Although there were two Officers on duty with me that day, only one made a lasting impression.

Correctional Officer Peters was an OG. He had at least ten years of seniority when I first worked with him. He was gruff, with a booming voice, laughed easily, and talked a lot of shit! He had an easy-going personality and could get the inmates to do what they were told. He was so jovial the majority of the time, it was hard for me to tell when he was being serious; and because he was a shit-talker by nature, I had to pay close attention to do so.

"Cromwell, pop cell 126," Officer Peters yelled.

I popped cell 126. He was searching even-numbered cells that day. He was in and out in the allotted fifteen minutes it should take to do a decent cell search. In addition to the cell searches, I continued to run the dayroom, and telephone programs.

"Close cell 126," he yelled. I closed the cell door and they moved on.

"Cromwell open cell 128," he yelled.

Once again, I popped the cell. The cell was opened, searched, and closed, then we moved on.

The trouble began when he yelled, "Cromwell, pop cell 130!" I popped the cell. Unbeknownst to me, one of the inmates housed in cell 130 was in the dayroom playing cards. When he heard his cell number called, he stood up and began slowly walking toward the cell.

"Hey, why are you searching my cell?" He asked Officer Peters.

"Because I fucking want to," he replied.

That response led to a heated exchange between the Officer and the inmate. The Officer was in the cell and had begun throwing things out of the cell door. Per CDCR policy, an inmate had the right to watch a search of his cell from a safe distance. As the cell search and verbal exchange continued between the Officer and the inmate, I walked closer to the control booth window to get a better view of the cell and to keep an eye on the situation. I was getting nervous. I removed my H&K from my back and held it loosely in my hands. My heartbeat quickened, I broke out in a cold sweat and my breathing slowed. "Oh Lord, please don't let me have to shoot someone today!" I silently prayed.

Before I knew it, the inmate had walked into the cell with the Officer. Was that allowed? I couldn't for the life of me remember what the post orders said. From my elevated position, I couldn't see inside the cell, as the cell was blocked by the B section stairs. I didn't know what was happening. All I could do was listen to the raised voices. Soon the inmate was backing out of the cell with his hands up, while Officer Peters had one hand on his chest, walking forward lightly pushing the inmate out of the cell. I distinctly heard the Officer say to the inmate.

"Motherfucker, don't make me tell her to shoot you!"

Who was the "she" he was referring to? Before I could figure it out, he yelled.

"Shoot him, Cromwell!" I racked a round. One in the chamber. My breathing became shallow.

Was I supposed to shoot an inmate if the Officer told me to? They reminded me of two bulls locking horns in the wild. Who would get the upper hand? Who would stand down? In the next few minutes which felt like an eternity, I would get the answer. The inmate stood down, and they both began laughing! What the hell just happened? The inmate picked through his discarded items, threw a few back into his cell, and went back to playing cards. Officer Peters began bagging up the contraband he retrieved from the cell search. I breathed a sigh of relief. It was over. After removing the magazine from my weapon, I removed the bullet from the chamber and placed it back in the magazine. Had I been punked? or hazed? I didn't know . . . and just like that, the dayroom program continued without missing a beat.

As my first shift came to an end, I locked up the housing unit dayroom. I also locked up the inmates who returned to the building from the recreational yard. I laid out my equipment to make it easier for the Officer who would relieve me to count it all. I was hoping my relief would do me the same courtesy and report at least thirty minutes early. With the day I had, I needed a nap, a drink, or both.

No luck, my relief came directly at 2:00 p.m. Just like the Officer I relieved that morning; I popped the door and was in the sally port in a nanosecond. I am sure I was halfway across the yard before he settled into his position. I had survived my first day. Welcome to prison, Bitch!

I loved being a PIE. As someone without a permanent position, I worked all over the Institution. It alleviated most of my responsibilities for the post. I simply did my job for that shift, and moved on to a new post the next day. Since I arrived at LAC before the installation of the electrified fence, the twelve guard towers were still active and would remain so for several years. I loved working the towers. I rotated through every tower. The position was perfect for me. I was isolated from inmates and staff alike because the towers are located outside the facilities, on the outside of the secure perimeter.

I enjoyed the seasons from my unique perch. I experienced the first winter snowfall in the guard towers. It was magical and made me almost forget I was in a Level IV men's prison. I avoided the scorching heat of the recreational yards in the summertime. It gave me time to think and contemplate my career and what I wanted to accomplish in the Department. I loved being cocooned in the safety of those towers. I hated when they were deactivated upon the activation of the electrified fence.

My PIE years quickly flew by. I worked every shift, every yard, and every assignment in the Institution. It allowed me to not only learn LAC but to learn CDCR. I liked some yards and assignments more than others. There were positions I loved, yards I preferred, and staff I enjoyed working with. Depending on whom I worked with, the shift could either fly by or drag on. After the guard tower, the Control Booth was my favorite position in the Institution.

During those early years, CDCR became my second family, a dysfunctional family, but a family, nonetheless. Not only did we work together, but on the weekends, we would often play together too. Sometimes we would meet at a local park for a game of volleyball, or somebody would have a cookout or a pool party in their backyard. There were spa days, shopping trips, parties at the surrounding nightclubs, and comedy central. We worked hard and played even harder!

I bet you didn't know that Correctional Officers have groupies. I don't know if it is the norm in all Institutions, but it certainly was at LAC. It was reminiscent of military towns. There wasn't much to do or anywhere of consequence to work in the Antelope Valley. It is considered a commuter's paradise. The cost of living is low, and Los Angeles is 60 miles south. Since the California Department of Corrections and Rehabilitation is one of the highest paying organizations in the State of California, Correctional Officers are very popular and often hotly pursued. Marriages were made and broken. Families were formed and children were born. My daughter lived her entire childhood while I worked for the Department. Prison life was all she knew.

When I was offered the opportunity to become full-time, I jumped at the chance. It would allow me to have a permanent shift and assignment. It would also give me a seniority number. Everything for an Officer was based on our seniority number. It determined who worked voluntary as well as involuntary overtime. It determined who would go home at the end of each shift if all positions weren't filled. Overtime was highly prized by staff. Depending on how much overtime you worked, you could more than double your annual salary. Many Officers earned up to $200,000 dollars annually simply based on how much overtime they worked. When

I became permanent full-time, I had the worst seniority number in the Institution. There was a formula that determined your seniority number. It was based on your date of hire, the Academy you attended that year, and when you reported to the Institution. If multiple cadets reported to the same Institution on the same date, then your social security number was used to determine what seniority number you were given. My seniority number was 508. I knew I had nothing coming. I was offered Facility C, Relief Officer with Tuesday and Wednesday off. I took it. A relief position gives you an assignment, but the assignment itself is to cover multiple positions as the assigned Officers took their regular days off. I didn't mind that position as it allowed me the opportunity to work multiple positions on the facility, including housing units, the yard, and the chow hall. During my years as a PIE, I discovered I enjoyed moving around.

I was excited to finally have a full-time position, but I was also a little apprehensive. I was looking forward to being permanent, but my new position was on Charlie yard.

CHAPTER 5

WELCOME TO JURASSIC PARK

Facility C or Charlie yard was the worst facility in the Institution. It earned its nickname "Jurassic Park" because it was a Level IV and the most violent yard of them all. There were multiple incidents on the facility, per shift, every day, sometimes even on First Watch. Fights, assaults, drugs, and weapons possession happened so often that the yard could be on a modified program or lockdown on any given day. Sometimes, it was so bad that the Warden would lock the yard down for weeks, sometimes months. A lockdown was so the facility could be thoroughly searched for drugs and weapons, and to give the inmates a cooling-off period.

During one particularly grueling lockdown that lasted several months, I was assigned to Third Watch, C3 Control Booth Officer. The staff was on edge after weeks and weeks of cell feeding and cleaning the buildings. The inmates were on edge due to being locked in their cells for 24 hours a day, for months at a time; barred from dayroom, yard, education, vocation, walking to chow, and all other programs.

Additionally, they were unable to make telephone calls or receive visits from their friends and families.

Yes, lockdowns served a purpose, but they were brutal. During lockdowns, there was little to no inmate movement. That meant, no porters, no clerks, and no cooks. When there weren't any inmates to cook or clean, it fell to the Officers to do the job.

Cell feeding was a long, tedious, sweaty, dirty, and nasty job. The staff cooked the food and schlepped it across the recreational yard, in big, hot metal carts, to each housing unit. Once there, Officers would have to open every food port in each cell, and pass trays through the portal to feed each inmate.

After cell feeding was complete, we would return to each housing unit to retrieve the food trays. Then clean the housing unit. It was dirty, thankless work. As you can imagine the inmates were usually stinky and dirty after having been locked in their cells for days, or weeks. They were also mean. They took every opportunity to demean and degrade us. They would call us their maids, servants, slaves, and much worse. Needless to say, the staff hated lockdowns as much, if not more than the inmates.

After 72 hours of lockdown, the Control Booth Officers were required, per policy, to shower each inmate, and every 72 hours thereafter. By the time I completed showering all 200 inmates in the housing unit, it would be time to start all over again. Day in and day out, week after week for as long as the lockdown continued.

Usually, you could hear a pin drop in the building on lockdowns. However, on one particular day, the inmates were restless and rowdy. They were yelling and screaming through the cell doors, throwing things out of their cells, fishing lines littered the floors (inmates would use makeshift lines to send and receive notes and contraband between the cells) and some were flooding their cells by putting things in their toilets. When they were on a particularly long lockdown they would lie, cheat and steal to get out of their cells. A trip across the facility for a disciplinary hearing in their minds allowed them to leave their cells to at least get some fresh air.

I'm not sure what transpired on Second Watch, but by the time I showed up for my shift, the housing unit was in full meltdown. Several cell fights broke out, responding staff utilized pepper spray and batons to quell the disturbances. That only served to hype the inmates up even more.

I started my shower program in A section as usual. I released two cells at a time, both upper and lower tiers. Each tier and each section had its designated shower. Once I opened a cell, each inmate was directed to the shower in his section. Both inmates in each cell were required to shower together and given ten minutes to do so. Unfortunately, within 30 minutes of starting my shower program that day, I sounded the building alarm. An inmate housed in cell 205 refused to return to his assigned cell upon completion of his shower. I utilized all my powers of persuasion, short of begging, to cajole him to return to his cell to no avail.

When all else failed, I pressed the building alarm, turned on the housing unit lights, opened both sally port doors, and awaited the calvary. Once the inmate heard the alarm, he sat down on the dayroom floor ready to assume the position. As staff began running in, I directed them to A section. Then I gave the Sergeant a quick synopsis of the issue. The inmate was quickly handcuffed and escorted out of the housing unit. Which, I am sure is just what he wanted. While the incident was happening, the inmates were yelling and screaming profanities from behind their cell doors. Upon completion of the incident, I turned off the housing unit lights, which seemed to always have a calming effect on the inmate population. I closed the sally port doors and continued my shower program. I completed A section. Then B section received their showers with relatively few issues or problems. However, as I began in C section, I noticed one inmate in cell 238 that was unusually agitated. He was cussing and carrying on, completely focused on me. He began calling me names, threatening me, and just being a general asshole. So, I made a big show of closing all the Control Booth windows. Hoping, that when he saw that and thought I couldn't hear him, he would quiet down. Of course, I could still hear him, but he didn't know that. It didn't work. He continued yelling for hours. Working in a violent, Level IV prison for as long as I had, I was frequently called everything but a child of God. The trick was to tune it out and ignore it as much as possible.

On the few occasions when I could not or did not want to ignore the disrespect there were methods I used to handle the situation. Sometimes, my response came via the building microphone and I gave as good as I got. Eventually, the inmate would stop after I talked about his mama, his family, and the size of his tiny penis. This was rare, and I only did it as a last resort. I didn't like how it made me feel. It made me feel like I was stooping to the inmate's level. Sometimes, the porters who worked for me in the building would check the inmate to the point that he would stop. The inmate would usually apologize all the while promising never to do it again. I never exactly knew what the porters said to him, but it would scare him enough to leave me alone. That is all I wanted.

Mostly, I would write the inmate up for disrespect. A Rules Violation Report (RVR) could make the inmate lose time and extend his sentence. However, that was a long and tedious process and did not have an immediate effect on the inmate, so it would have little to no impact in the moment. The final method and the one I used the most in that scenario was to announce over the building loudspeaker that his cell door was "broken" and I could not open it. Therefore, he would not get a shower or anything else for that matter. If he fucked with me, I would fuck with him. I would skip his cell altogether and continue my shower program.

Usually, by the time I got five cells down, that inmate would be appropriately contrite, apologetic, and begging to be let out for a shower, or at least to let his cellmate out. Not this time. He became more enraged, and the level of disrespect ratcheted up to a 10. "You ugly, stupid bitch!" he screamed. "Fuck you and your bitch ass mama!" He continued, hour after hour, while I completed my shower program.

I was every kind of bitch and hoe that day: a stupid bitch, a dumb bitch, and an ugly hoe. I had heard it all before, but after that unrelenting siege, it began to take its toll on me. I was frazzled. The end of my shift could not come fast enough. I would need a few glasses of wine and a bath when I got home. I felt dirty.

At approximately 9:30 p.m., thirty minutes before I could make my escape, the Sergeant let himself into my housing unit, using the side door. He didn't call in advance. He didn't let me know he was coming, which is common courtesy and unwritten protocol.

"Cromwell, pop me up," he said.

I opened the sally port doors and let him into my Control Booth. I had no idea why he was there and was a little curious.

I had known the Sergeant for years. I even attended his church on the odd Sunday. We were friends. Maybe he came to comfort me? Nah, that is not what we do in prison.

"Hey, Sarge, what's up?" I greeted him. He began.

"Cromwell, now you know per CDCR policy, you have to shower every inmate every seventy-two hours. I was told you didn't shower the inmates in cell 238."

I don't know who the hell narced me out, but I would make it my business to find out. Did they also tell him how the inmate cursed me out, threatened me, and was an asshole for hours? Was he kidding me! Before he could utter another word, my shoulders slumped defeatedly, and the dam broke. I began to cry.

Through my tears I said, "Sarge, I swear to God, if you make me give that inmate a shower tonight, I will give you my badge and quit this damn job," voice shaking, tears running down my face.

I tried to hold back, but it was impossible. The nerve . . . the unmitigated gall. Who did he think he was! I continued, "After all the bitches and hoes I have been called today?" my voice rising, "I swear if you don't get the hell out of my Control Booth right now . . ."

Before I could complete my sentence, he yelled, "Okay, okay, okay, pop me out, pop me out!" And I did. He left through the same side door he came through. My relief finally arrived, as I was drying my tears and pulling myself together. I left there almost running, trying to decide if I would be returning tomorrow.

I went home, and soaked in the bathtub until I was a prune. I drank the entire bottle of wine. I fell into a good wine-induced sleep. I was groggy when I woke up the next day. I put on my uniform and boots and went to work to do it all again. Thank goodness it was a better day. I still didn't know if I wanted to do the job anymore. Thankfully, gratefully, when I reported to my Control Booth the Sergeant had removed the offending inmate from my building and transferred him to another yard. During my shift, I wrote the inmate a Rules Violation Report (RVR) for disrespect. If nothing else, he might think better next time while he was serving his additional three months that RVR would add to his sentence. All was right in my world, at least for the time being anyway.

Walking across the recreational yard when the yard was out was like walking the gauntlet. As a female, I was constantly and continually sexually harassed. The inmates were unabashedly unafraid to undress you with their eyes. They would leer at you and say some of the most disgusting things about your hair, face, and body. I loathed walking across the yard when inmates were out. Unfortunately, they were usually out, as I worked Third Watch and the recreational yard was from 12:30 p.m. to 3:00 p.m.

every day. I developed a system to avoid walking across the yard alone, to get to my building with as little harassment as possible. I pretended that my shades were my full armor. As long as I was wearing them and the inmates could not see my eyes, I felt a small level of protection. I would arrive early, sign-in, then sit on the bench outside the program office to await an escort. Of course, Officers don't have escorts. My fellow male Officers were unaware that frequently they were mine. I would wait for my assigned partner of the day, or instead of him, any other male Officer who was walking across the yard close enough to my building to drop me off. I did that almost every day I was assigned to Charlie yard. Unfortunately, it didn't always work. Somedays, I would have to walk across the yard on my own.

One day while rushing to work, I forgot my shades, my protective armor. I didn't realize it until I walked onto the yard. As I was signing in that day, on the verge of tears, the Sergeant noticed and asked me what was wrong. I tearfully explained my system and told him I would have to go back to my car to retrieve my shades. He looked at me for a minute, as if he was trying to make sense of what I told him. He took the shades off his face, shoved them at me, and yelled, "Go to work!" And I did.

Black inmates were the worst. They always gave me the hardest time. They were the ones who would be quick to call me names, sexually harass me, and generally be disrespectful, but it was also Black inmates that often came to my rescue. It was my theory that the former, inevitably hated themselves, probably hated their mothers and women in general. The latter were happy to have some estrogen present to dilute all the testosterone found in prison. Once, early in my career when I was the Chow Hall Officer, there was a White Officer who was short and curt with me every time we had a conversation. One day, he called me a bitch in front of my inmate workers. I was so shocked I couldn't respond. When he left the chow hall, the shot caller asked me if we were "playing." I told him I did not play like that. A few days later, the same Officer came back to my work site. He groveled and profusely apologized. I don't know if the inmates had anything to do with his apology, but I didn't have any more problems with him.

Many times, throughout my career, an inmate, usually one of my clerks or porters, warned me if something was going down in the housing unit or on the recreational yard. They would tell me what was happening in my building, who were the shot callers, the soldiers, and the followers. Which prison gang controlled the building, including the drugs and weapons. Sometimes they would tell me what Officers were disrespectful, racists, and all-around assholes. They would tell me which Officers were on the verge of being beaten down if they didn't adjust their attitude. Ultimately, inmates knew everything happening in the facility because they lived there and not having their ear to the street could mean big trouble.

I continued to work all over Charlie yard for a solid year. The frequency of incidents could wear you down. Many times while walking across the yard, the yard alarm would sound. When a yard alarm sounded, the inmates on the facility, regardless of their location, or what they were doing were required to assume the position and sit on the ground. If it was a bad incident, they were required to lie on their stomachs. The policy was to protect responding staff as they ran to the alarm location. It kept inmates from getting in the way and slowing down the response.

One day there was a fight on the yard. The responding staff, including a female Sergeant, quickly responded and quelled the disturbance. The Officers broke up the fight. While they were escorting the inmates across the yard, an inmate sitting on the ground closest to the Sergeant, quickly got up, punched her in the face, and just as quickly sat back down. The yard alarm was activated again and every Officer in the vicinity dog-piled on top of that inmate. The inmate did not struggle at all. The rest of us ran to assist the Sergeant who was struggling to her feet. We forced her to sit back down as we awaited a medical response. The inmate was quickly handcuffed and carried across the yard to be placed in a holding cell and re-housed in Administrative Segregation for Assault on a Peace Officer.

The medical team responded and carried the Sergeant, via stretcher, to the medical facility. She was eventually transported to an outside hospital via ambulance for medical evaluation.

The word on the yard was the inmate owed a large drug debt and could not repay it. He had to get off the yard. If he didn't get off the yard there would be a green light on him. A green light was permission to assault or kill an inmate on sight.

When the yard went down that day, he saw his opportunity, and the poor Sergeant was the scapegoat. That was the scariest part of the job. The possibility of being assaulted or worse. I always vowed that if I was ever assaulted, that would be it for me. I would quit and find another job.

Women make better Correctional Officers than men. My opinion is based on my experiences, as well as a myriad of reasons. First, we are mothers, we raise children and are comfortable giving people orders, guiding their choices, and disciplining them when needed and necessary. Second, we have years of experience manipulating men, our fathers, husbands, partners, and sons. It is not a stretch for us to know how to manipulate most inmates. Women are better communicators. Most of the time we can easily get them to do want we want.

Third, we do not usually lead with our egos. Male Officers are usually ego-driven. It generally happens when men are dealing with each other. It often becomes a pissing contest. A pissing contest that usually leads to disrespect, coupled with aggression, typically leads to an assault or physical altercation.

However, there is something to be said about the sheer brute force and physicality of men, which is often needed in a men's prison. No matter how much we are willing to de-escalate a situation, many times, inmates had to be forced to comply.

In that case, women are less effective. Physically we are smaller in stature and therefore, less intimidating. We are always at a physical disadvantage and inmates are well aware of that. Unfortunately, for the Sergeant that day, the inmate used it to his advantage.

CHAPTER 6

MY FRIEND, REVA

Officer Reva and I were best friends. We met when she transferred to LAC from Ironwood State Prison. She joined the Department four years before me and had already earned two hash marks to my one. Each hash mark indicated three years of service. We would nod as we passed each other on the roadway en route to our respective work assignments. Eventually, we found ourselves both working on "Jurassic Park."

I was the Control Booth Officer in Housing Unit 3. She was the Floor Officer in Housing Unit 5. We had everything in common. We were both Black women, divorced, single mothers who worked a tough male-dominated job on a Level IV yard, in a men's prison. We were members of a very small, unique girls club. We became fast friends. She was sweet, soft-spoken, and very funny. Her personality did not seem to jive with being a badass prison guard, but a badass prison guard, she was, nonetheless. She quickly became the yin to my yang. We worked together and spent most of our days off together as well. I considered her my sister. Everything seemed to solidify our sisterhood. Our kids, her son, and my daughter went to the same high school and were friends too. In addition to spending most of our days off together, we often vacationed and spent most holidays together. When you saw me, she was usually in tow, and vice versa.

We both worked Third Watch; 2:00 p.m.–10:00 p.m. with Tuesdays/ Wednesdays off. While at work in the evenings, after chow, during institutional count we would rotate going to each other's housing unit to eat dinner together as often as possible.

Usually, she would come to my Control Booth. Since she was a Floor Officer, once she completed her count, she was relatively free and mobile until the count cleared and the evening program began. Occasionally, I could get one of my co-workers to relieve me and I would go to her housing unit, although not often. It was hard for me to go to her housing unit because my Control Booth position was not mobile.

Reva was close friends with Officer Felicity. She also worked Third Watch, but was assigned to Facility D. Since she didn't work on our facility, she could not eat dinner with us in the evenings. Officer Felicity was much younger, a little rougher, and harder than Reva. I was introduced to her during one of our many outings. She wasn't necessarily my cup of tea, but any friend of Reva's was a friend of mine.

We became known as the three musketeers around the Institution. On our days off we were typically together, whether we were at each other's houses, at the local park, or shopping together. Sometimes, we would host joint parties at my house. We enjoyed being together.

Since we did shift work, it was difficult to form close relationships with people who didn't work in the Department. Additionally, it could be a mean, difficult job where you could be assaulted and/or killed any day you went to work. Nobody else understood like another woman who also walked the toughest beat in the state. I am sure that solidified our bond even more. We could honestly talk about anything, including the difficulties of being women, working in a men's prison. We had each other's backs. The Department of Corrections and Rehabilitation was a good old boys club. So, we formed a club of our own.

Unfortunately, during that time I began having some issues with my daughter. She was a good kid, but puberty was difficult. I was a working, single mother, and she was a latchkey kid. Every day after school she arrived home to an empty house. She was expected to do her homework, eat the dinner I'd cooked her before I left for work, put the dishes in the dishwasher, lock up the house, and go to sleep at the appointed time. I knew it was a major responsibility for a middle school kid, but I was divorced and didn't have many options. Besides, she only had to do it three days a week. I had two days off, and on the weekends I would send her to my mother's house.

When you work on a prison yard, it is difficult to make a phone call outside the Institution. There was very few available outside telephone lines, for obvious reasons. The closest outside line was across the recreational yard in the Sergeant's office. As a Control Booth Officer, if I wanted to make a telephone call, I would have to beg one of my co-workers for relief and walk across the yard.

Leaving your position to make personal phone calls was frowned upon. The Facility Sergeant didn't like it, and he was my direct Supervisor. Therefore, I couldn't do it often.

The rule I had for my daughter, was that she would go straight home from school and no company was allowed in the house in my absence. She was required to answer my telephone calls when I randomly called to check on her. It wasn't the best solution, but because she was such a good kid, I thought it was a perfect plan.

One day, she didn't answer when I called. I was frantic. I made up an excuse to leave work early because I couldn't concentrate until I checked on her.

Unfortunately, for her, that was the day she'd decided to have a party. When I walked into my house in full uniform, all hell broke loose. Kids were running out of doors and jumping out of windows. They couldn't get out of there fast enough. Of course, they thought I was the police, and of course, I allowed them to think that. I began yelling and screaming that I was going to arrest them and call their parents. They couldn't get out of my house fast enough. My daughter was there alone to take the blame. What that incident showed me was that my fourteen-year-old daughter needed more direct supervision, and I needed a shift change. Too many of my peers had kids that went down the wrong path due to little to no parental supervision and too much time on their hands. I was not going to let that happen to my daughter.

Fortunately, it didn't take too much to convince my Sergeant that I needed a job change. I changed from Third Watch to First Watch, 10:00 p.m. to 6:00 a.m. overnights. It would allow me to go to work after my daughter was asleep for the night. She slept at my mother's house. My mother lived around the corner from us. I would go home, shower, pick her up from my mother's house and take her to school each morning. I was satisfied with the job change, but it didn't allow me the freedom to hang out with my friends any longer. That was a small price I was willing to pay for my kid.

One night, about three months later, while I was working in my post in Charlie 3 Control Booth, I received a letter. I was directed to report to The Office of Internal Affairs for an interview. I was under investigation for over-familiarity with an inmate. To say I was shocked would be an understatement. I was scared and confused. I knew I had not been overfamiliar with an inmate, but my heart sank, nonetheless. I had a sneaking suspicion I knew what was going on.

When I got off work the next morning, I called a few of my close, trusted friends. I asked them to meet me at Reva's apartment. When I arrived, they were already there. When I looked around, I saw Reva on the floor crying, with Felicity pacing back and forth. My other friends had looks of resignation on their faces. I had a lump in my throat and my stomach was in knots.

"What did you do?" I screamed as I walked into her apartment. She continued crying without answering me. At that moment I knew. It was her. She was having an illegal, illicit affair with an inmate, and because we were best friends, I was guilty by association.

"Why?" I asked. I wasn't expecting an answer because what could she say? There was never a good answer in such circumstances. Through her tears, she quietly said, "But I love him!" And there it was. Damn! "Why didn't you love yourself and your kids more?" I yelled at her. Knowing it was a rhetorical question she could not answer. I stood there sad and disappointed, wondering how we got here. Reva told me the whole sordid story.

"Why didn't you tell me before I was served by Internal Affairs?" I asked.

"They served you?" she asked incredulously. "I'm so sorry. I didn't know how to tell you, and I didn't think you'd understand," she continued.

Before I left her apartment that morning, it was decided that she would not return to the prison and that her correctional career was over. She would fax in her resignation. It was imperative to do it that way so she wouldn't be fired and could get a job to support herself and her children in the future. However, Felicity decided against our advice and went back to work. She stayed just long enough to go out on stress citing, "a hostile work environment." She attempted to prolong the inevitable so she could continue getting a paycheck for as long as possible. It didn't work and she eventually resigned. I thought we were friends, sisters even. I never spoke to Reva and Felicity again after that day. They had made their choice. We'd planned to be best friends forever, raise our children together, promote through the ranks together, and always have each other's backs. None of that would happen now.

Although I was exhausted, instead of going straight home that morning, I went to my mother's house. It was earlier than usual, but I knew she would be up reading her Bible. I don't know if it was the slump of my shoulders or a mother's intuition, but she knew what I needed.

"Are you in trouble?" She asked.

"No, but my friends are," I answered.

I laid my head on her bosom and cried like a baby. She comforted me. She hugged me, and prayed for me. She didn't just give me what I came for. She gave me what I needed. Then she sent me back into the world.

Inmates were always trying to entice us. It wasn't unusual to find hand-made roses, cards, and letters on our desks or in our lunch bags. Often, they would try to push the envelope even further. If you were a Control Booth Officer, like I was, sometimes when they showered, they would leave the lights on in hopes of enticing you. Quite frequently, they would masturbate in their cells, with the lights on, in full view.

When I worked overtime counting inmates in the housing units on First Watch, I would hold my keys close to my belt, trying to make as little noise as possible, as I made my way from cell to cell. Often, if they knew I was making my rounds, they would sometimes twist themselves into odd configurations to ensure I saw them naked or masturbating. That could also be a catch-22, because if they didn't hear me coming, I would catch them having sex with each other. Either way, it was disgusting. I was just trying to do my job, but it felt like dodging a minefield.

When I would report an incident to my Supervisor or write the inmate a Rules Violation Report, I would often get chastised for not being tough enough. If I had a dime for every time a male Supervisor said to me, "Cromwell, they are men, what do you expect in a men's prison?" I never knew if they actually expected an answer to the question or if they were just talking out of the side of their necks.

Central Control was the checkpoint for Facilities A and B. When I arrived the Sergeant said over the loudspeaker, in front of all the staff arriving for the day, as well as, all the inmates arriving for their daily work assignments, "Cromwell, are you supposed to be here?" My stomach dropped. I squared my shoulders.

"Unless you know something I don't, I'm here to go to work," I replied. I saw her pick up the telephone. A bead of sweat trickled down my back. I swear I could hear the clock ticking on the wall. It felt like hours. I stood there humiliated in front of my peers and inmates alike. After a few minutes, she opened the sally port, handed me my equipment and I proceeded to my assignment.

At that moment my feelings about the Department changed. My Supervisors and peers had become my judge and jury. They created a hostile work environment and made it unpleasant for me to work there. Over the next several days, the prison had several meetings with all staff, under threat of disciplinary action before the rumor mill would stop. I'm sure they were afraid of a lawsuit. A few of my well-meaning friends advised me to go out on stress. I could have, but I refused. The Department was my chosen career, and nobody was going to push me out, especially for something I did not do.

When everything had somewhat died down, the Sergeant told me about an incident that had preceded the "Reva Debacle" as I would come to call it. One day when Reva reported to work, the inmate was waiting for her at the gate. The two of them slowly walked across the yard to the housing unit, in front of staff and inmates, while talking and laughing along the way. It looked like a date. She then allowed him to escort her into the housing unit, which was never done.

Unless an inmate worked for you, there was no reason for him to be in the sally port with staff. It was an unwritten rule.

The Sergeant had a meeting with her later that day about her blatant behavior. He told her it was not a good look. He gave her a direct order to stop. Of course, she protested and said she wasn't doing anything wrong. She ignored him. It didn't take long before she was under investigation. There were wild rumors about her having sex with the inmate in the housing unit. I'm not sure if that was ever proven. As a Correctional Officer, sworn to uphold the law, everything Reva did deeply offended my moral compass. I later heard through the institutional grapevine, that Reva had moved to Sacramento and married her inmate lover.

My experience with Reva changed me forever. It changed how I thought about my colleagues and how I operated for the rest of my career. I would never let myself get so close to another person that their actions could negatively impact my career.

There were rumors that Reva was the victim of domestic abuse. I would often wonder if she regretted her choice. Time marched on and like so many things, Reva faded into the recesses of my life. I ran into her many, many years later. She looked the same. Our conversation was brief. I told her I missed her. She said she missed me too. We hugged and walked away. It was one of the saddest moments of my life. Two old friends . . . now two complete strangers.

Reva was the first friend in my career who resigned while under investigation for having a sexual relationship with an inmate. Sadly, she was not the last.

When female Officers succumbed to the advances of an inmate, it felt like a kick in the gut. They chose a convicted felon over the sisterhood. It made us all look bad. It was a disservice to and denigrated all the women who had broken the barriers so we could be there. That was the last time I saw Reva. We were no longer sisters. We had chosen different paths.

The Reva incident would rear its ugly head several times throughout the years. Every time I advanced in my career, the rumors would start up briefly and I would hear them. "There goes Cromwell," they'd whisper. "She was involved with an inmate, and got away with it," they would say. I didn't let it stop me. It didn't waylay me. After all, I had a 25-year career to finish, and I was just getting started.

CHAPTER 7

INCARCERATED FAMILY AND FRIENDS

I worked on Delta yard on and off throughout my career. During that time, the facility transitioned through a multitude of missions. It seemed like every few years or so we would be required to learn something new. When the prison opened Facility D was a Level IV general population yard. Later, it added the Reception Center (RC), housing all new inmates recently incarcerated from Los Angeles County in Housing Unit 1. Most men arrested in Los Angeles County and sentenced to prison were housed there.

In the Reception Center, inmates wore orange jumpsuits, until they completed the classification process, which is designed to identify their current offense and determine their skills, education level, health concerns, prior offenses, and gang affiliation. The Reception Center is where their points are calculated, which determines where they can be appropriately housed, whether at LAC or other Institutions throughout the State. It is also where it would be determined if an inmate had relatives and/or friends who work for the Department of Corrections and Rehabilitation.

Sometimes it worked, sometimes it didn't. If it didn't work the employee was responsible for informing the Institution.

An incarcerated family and friends form is required from all correctional staff when joining the Department. Like everybody else, I completed the form during the application process. If it was determined you failed to notify the Department, you could be fired for being less than honest. How would they know your intentions? There were cases of family members joining the Department who were gang members or gang sympathizers to do the gangs' bidding and to introduce drugs and contraband into the Institution.

Once the form is submitted, it is placed in your employee file, hopefully never to be seen again, if you are lucky. Well, I wasn't that lucky. Several times throughout my career, unfortunately, I have encountered a family member or friend on a yard or in a housing unit. Usually out of the blue and without prior notice. Typically, while minding my business.

I wasn't concerned about the odd inmate with whom I may have gone to elementary school or may have known me from the neighborhood church. What could they say? They knew me and/or my family when I was a child? So. Big deal. That would not earn them any brownie points. That information wasn't worth anything.

The ones that could be problematic were the ones who knew me well. Or the ones who knew intimate details about my family. Of course, relatives were the worst. They could be dangerous. They could try to parlay their knowledge, somehow to their benefit. They would try to get something from you. Perhaps tell the inmate population something you didn't want them to know. Something personal, something embarrassing. If all else failed, they could try to set you up. Attempted extortion or blackmail was a distinct possibility. Who needs that kind of problem? I certainly didn't. Although I had not lived there since I was a child, I was still from L.A. so I should have known it was inevitable.

Through our family grapevine, I kept track of who was in and out of prison. Who sold drugs and who had a dubious "career." But it was just a matter of time.

When it began happening, I was still surprised. Periodically, while walking across the recreational yard, I would hear an unidentifiable inmate yell my entire name. It had begun happening so frequently that I would barely slow down or break my stride. I certainly never looked around to see who it was. Inmates are barred from using your first name unless you gave them permission. Since I had never given an inmate permission to use my first name, I knew it was probably someone who knew me from my childhood. It never really presented a problem, until one day it did.

Out of the blue, inmates began coming up to me asking if I was from a specific street in Los Angeles. I would always lie and say I was from the exact opposite side of town. The inmates could not have that information unless someone told them. It began happening more and more frequently.

One day, I was working on Facility D as a Yard Officer. During chow release, I entered the Reception Center in Housing Unit 1. When I walked to C section to release that side of the building for chow, my first cousin, Tad stepped out of his cell in an orange jumpsuit. The orange jumpsuit indicated that he was new to the Institution and had yet to go through the classification process. When inmates first arrived at the Reception Center, they were given an orange jumpsuit and were only given their chambray shirt and blue jeans upon completion of the classification process. The classification process could take up to 120 days.

He smiled as he walked past me, as he continued to chow. I was a little shocked and taken aback. My mind began racing. It took me a few minutes to shake it off and continue with chow release.

Tad's mother and my father were siblings. He was my aunt's oldest son and he was several years older than me, so we never moved in the same familial circles. He was from my oldest sister's generation, so I didn't know much about him, other than he began going in and out of Institutions as a kid, in group homes, Juvenile Halls, and eventually state prisons. I thought about the encounter with my cousin overnight, trying to decide what I should do. I know what I was supposed to do, but was it really necessary?

I knew because he was from Los Angeles County depending on the classification process he could be housed at LAC. If he stayed at LAC, it would make it easier for my family to visit him. I decided that if he didn't say anything neither would I. After all, he was an OG and knew how to play the game.

When I arrived at work the next day, and upon completion of the morning meal, I made a beeline to Housing Unit 1. He was standing alone in C section. I walked up to him. Just a Correctional Officer walking up to a random inmate. "If you don't say anything, I won't say anything either," I said. I didn't wait for a response. I turned on my heels and just as quickly walked out of the building.

Things quieted down for a while. No more inmates walked up to me with unnecessary information. Apparently, it was working.

One day I was at work minding the business that pays me in Housing Unit 1. I was working all over the Institution and had not been on Delta yard in several weeks. I was standing in the dayroom when my cousin Tad quickly walked up to me with a worried look on his face. Although I had no idea what his problem was, a knot formed in my stomach.

"I need your help," he said. I didn't respond.

"If you don't help me, they're going to hurt me," he continued. There it was, the setup. I didn't respond. I quickly left the building and went straight to the Sergeant's office. I simply told him that I had just run into my first cousin in Housing Unit 1. He sent me to the Custody Captain's office to write a memorandum. I was redirected to another yard for the remainder of my shift that day. The next time I was assigned to Facility D, Housing Unit 1, my cousin Tad was long gone.

TITLE 15, 3406

Committed Relative and Friends of Employees

If an employee becomes aware that any relative or person with whom the employee has or has had either a personal or business relationship, has been committed to or transferred to the jurisdiction of the Department, the employee shall notify in writing, the employee's Institution head or appropriate director/ assistant secretary of that fact.

I wish I could say that was my last encounter with an incarcerated family member or friend, but that would be too easy. And my career was anything but easy.

One summer my oldest teenage nephew came to spend the summer with me. Primarily to get a break from his mother, my sister, but also to babysit my daughter for the summer. I no longer allowed her to stay home alone, but she staunchly refused to go to my mother's house. I didn't have the strength to argue and since I couldn't force her, I sent for my nephew instead. It was a welcomed change for both of us. I loved and missed him. I was working so much, I hadn't seen him in quite a while. My daughter was happy, my nephew was happy, and so was I. All was well in our world.

After completing my shift one day, I grabbed my lunch bag and began walking across the recreational yard. I had a pep in my step because it was my Friday, which was really Tuesday, and I couldn't wait to start my weekend. "Hey Cromwell," they would call as I walked across the yard. I didn't even slow down. I was on a mission to get the heck across that yard and to get home as fast as I could. So, I walked faster. One inmate, off to my right side said, "Hey Cromwell, long time no see!" I continued walking; unsure I heard him correctly. He continued a little louder this time. "How is your sister?" That stopped me dead in my tracks. I was sure I heard him correctly that time.

I knew who it was before our eyes even met. It was my nephew's father. He was my sister's childhood sweetheart. What were the odds? We grew up together in our gritty South Central neighborhood in Los Angeles. I hadn't seen him in quite a few years, probably since I was a teenager. Now, he was a grown man, but he still had that little boy face, I remembered. When he smiled, he still had the gold tooth he had since seventh grade.

Like so many of the boys from our neighborhood, his path in life seemed to be pre-ordained. Most of them were high school dropouts. They joined the drug trade that proliferated in our neighborhoods in the 1980s. Then, they were in and out of prison, until they finally caught a case and struck out, with life in prison for a drug offense.

"Hey Chase, how are you doing?" I asked. He quickly fell in step with me, as I continued walking.

"I didn't know you worked here." He said.

"Yep," I responded.

"What are you doing here? The last I heard; you were paroled."

He smiled, "I did, but you know, I'm always doing the wrong thing."

"Yea, it looks like it. Well, it was good seeing you again!" I said, trying to get to that gate. Was it good seeing him? Not like this.

"How's that boy of mine?"

"Oh, he's fine. Everybody's fine." I waved him off as I finally arrived at the yard gate. I was on my way home. I already knew I didn't plan on writing a memo. I would just avoid working overtime on Delta yard.

On my way home, I wrestled with whether or not I should tell my teenage nephew that I ran into his father on a prison yard. By the time I arrived home, I'd decided I would tell him. I felt it was a cautionary tale. What could happen if he made the wrong turn. If he made a bad decision. In America, Black boys very rarely got a second chance. No grace. If he slipped up and made one mistake, one bad decision, where his father currently resided could be his future. I thought if nothing else it could be a teachable moment.

"Hey Chase," I began. He was his father's namesake.

"Guess who I ran into at work today?"

"Who?" he replied.

"Your father," I said.

"Really? I thought he was up North!"

"You knew he was back in prison?"

"Yep, I send him letters."

The pit in my stomach returned. "You do?" I was trying, but failing to sound casual. "Does he write you back?"

"Yea, I just got a letter last week!" He ran to his room to retrieve the letter.

Just as I suspected, the last letter had my forwarding address on it. Letters from an inmate at my Institution had begun arriving at my house. This was going to be a problem.

"Why didn't you tell me?"

"Because we have been writing on and off for years, and I didn't think about it." With that, he went back to playing his video game. It was definitely a problem.

My nephew certainly had the right to correspond with his father, and his father had the right to correspond with him, but now I was in the middle, and I wasn't willing to do anything to jeopardize my job. I remembered how that situation with my cousin Tad had turned out.

The next day at work, I pulled Chase's central file. As I suspected, he was sentenced to 25 years to life for a drug offense. He had been in and out of prison beginning in his late teens and consequently had a rap sheet a mile long. He was also a drug addict and couldn't seem to stay clean long enough to get his life together. So, the last time he was arrested on a drug possession charge was his last time. He struck out. He would spend the rest of his life in prison.

I submitted my memorandum to the Custody Captain informing him about the family friend that was housed on Facility D. Nothing changed, but at least I had done what I was required to do. I continued working Delta yard on and off for the next several months. I never encountered Chase again. I assumed he completed the classification process and was sent on his way to his receiving Institution. My nephew stayed with me for the remainder of that summer. We never discussed his father again.

CHAPTER 8

THREE STRIKES AND YOU'RE OUT!

In 1993, the three-strikes law originated in Washington State. It set the standard for such laws across the United States. Its primary purpose was to increase the safety of the general public by ensuring the most violent offenders were imprisoned for life. The Washington law meant any person convicted of two violent felonies before sentencing for their new crime, would receive a mandatory sentence of life in prison.

In 1994, President Bill Clinton signed the Violent Crime Control and Law Enforcement Act. It was known as the "Crime Bill." The three-strikes provision was included in the bill. It made it easier for each state to adopt its version of the law. The bill provided funding for more Police Officers as well as more courts. It allowed the courts to apply longer sentences to decrease the number of repeat offenders. Its intent was to make criminal sentencing easier and to restore the general public's trust in the criminal justice system.

It also increased the incarceration rate and proliferation of prisons across the country, especially in the State of California.

In 1994, California voters enacted the most stringent version of the three-strikes law. It was directly in response to the murders of Kimber Reynolds and Polly Klass. The California law imposed a life sentence for almost any crime, no matter how minor. If the perpetrator had two prior convictions for crimes defined as serious or violent by the California penal code. The law was originally intended for the most heinous crimes, (i.e. rape, murder, kidnapping, etc.) and to keep the most violent offenders behind bars. However, the California version of the law gave judges the ability to determine how the law was applied. As a result, most California inmates sentenced under the three-strikes law were mostly drug and non-violent offenders. Almost one-quarter of those incarcerated in the California prison system are convicted of drug offenses.

In 1992, Kimber Reynolds was 18 years old. She was out one night, in the Towers area of Fresno, California. When she was leaving the restaurant, she was robbed at gunpoint and murdered for absolutely no reason. The two men who murdered her were repeat offenders, with long histories of violent, as well as non-violent crimes. The gunman had been released from prison just two months before, having served time for auto theft. He was killed by the Police, but his accomplice was apprehended. He was tried and convicted of the murder. Even then, he wasn't given a life sentence. He was sentenced to nine years in prison. He would only be sentenced to life in prison over a decade later when he was convicted of domestic violence.

Mike Reynolds, Kimber's father, promised her on her deathbed that he would do everything in his power to not let her death be in vain. He became the face of the three-strikes law movement. He did not stop until the law was passed.

In 1993, Polly Klass was just twelve years old when she was abducted at knifepoint from her home in Petaluma, California during a slumber party with her friends. The man who raped, murdered, and buried her confessed. He had previous convictions for burglary, assault, and kidnapping. He was sentenced to sixteen years in prison on a prior conviction but was released early on parole.

While on parole, he murdered Polly. He was convicted of the crime and sentenced to death.

The original intent of the law was honorable, however, California's law was not drafted correctly because it allowed those convicted of what would be considered non-violent felonies to be sentenced to prison for life.

By the time I joined the Department of Corrections and Rehabilitation, the three-strikes law was in effect.

In 1994, California had twenty-six prisons, but over the next decade, it would increase the number of prisons to a total of thirty-five. Now, California has one of the highest incarceration rates in America. The majority of inmates incarcerated in the California prison system are men of color. In part, due to the mass incarceration of Black men, racism in the criminal justice system, and the mistreatment of the crack epidemic that impacted poor communities; as well as communities of color. I understood it first-hand as my nephew's father was struck out and sentenced to 25 to life in prison on a non-violent drug offense.

California became a prison state and one of the biggest employers. During that time, the Department increased its recruitment efforts because you need people to staff Institutions. Working in the prison system became one of the best-kept secrets in California.

The State's prison system was always overcrowded; however, it became so over-crowded that the Institutions began housing inmates in non-traditional areas such as dayrooms and gymnasiums. The ratio of inmates to staff increased. As a result, staff safety was jeopardized. The Correctional Officer Union sued the State of California due to massive overcrowding. As a result of the lawsuit, each housing unit received an additional Floor Officer. The Supreme Court determined the overcrowded prison system violated inmates' rights, and ordered the prisons to decrease their population.

As a Correctional Counselor, my caseload was replete with mostly Black and Brown inmates who were serving life sentences for drugs, as well as, minor non-violent offenses. It wasn't unusual for me to read an inmate's central file and discover life sentences for stealing low-budget items; such as pizzas and perm kits, as well as minor offenses such as receiving stolen property. The one case that haunts me still is the inmate who was serving twenty-five years to life for failure to appear at his court hearing. When I asked the inmate how in the world was he struck out for failure to appear? He said, "I was poor and Black and couldn't afford an attorney. So, I was given a public defender. When he told me he would handle my court hearing and I didn't need to appear, I believed him, but the joke was on me." It conceptualized the human cost and failure of the three-strikes law.

It is estimated that the law costs the state billions of dollars. Not to mention the cost of lost potential, losses in the job market, and losses to families and communities.

Since the law was first enacted in 1993, more than half the states in America have passed their version of the law.

CHAPTER 9

MY FIRST PROMOTION

After the Reva debacle, I sat on First Watch in C3 Control Booth for a year, brooding. I was licking my wounds. I was also avoiding as much contact as possible with staff and my peers. I heard what they were saying about me. My so-called friends went to great lengths to make sure I knew. Many of them thought I not only knew what was transpiring but that I was a willing participant. Of course, it wasn't true, but they didn't care. Gossip is rarely true. It doesn't have to be. As long as it was juicy, that was all they cared about.

Although I was good at it, I didn't particularly love being a Correctional Officer. The job required too many menial tasks. It required too much direct inmate contact. Cell searches and passing out toilet paper and tooth powder were not something I wanted to spend the rest of my life doing.

Being a Correctional Officer was the first rung on the correctional ladder. I was smart, ambitious and wanted more. I felt there was so much more I could do. There was one Sergeant I looked up to. She was always trying to encourage me. That was the thing I liked about her most. She had a profound effect on the course of my career, without even knowing it. One day she casually said, "So what are you going to do Cromwell, just stay at the bottom? I think you are too smart for that!" That one sentence was like a shot in my gut. It hit me deeply. It continually played over and over in my head. I just had to figure out what I was going to do about it.

When I first joined the Department of Corrections and Rehabilitation, I already had a plan. I intended to be a Correctional Counselor. The only reason I became a Correctional Officer in the first place, was to eventually be a Counselor. To be a Correctional Counselor, I was required to be an Officer for two years before I could apply for the position. Although I never wanted to be an Officer, I thought two years was a small price to pay to ultimately get the job I wanted.

After I met the two-year requirement, I began applying for the position. At LAC, the process required me to first get an acting position, so I could learn how to do the job before I could even be considered for the position. I applied to every Correctional Counselor II (CCII) Supervisor at the Institution. The CCII classification directly supervised Correctional Counselors. They could choose their staff. It was great for them. But not necessarily fair to everyone else.

After applying to each CCII without so much as a response, I went over their heads and applied to each Facility Captain, their direct Supervisor. I wasn't sure if that was the best course of action. I could have been shooting myself in the foot, but I was desperate. I felt like I was losing myself a little more each day I stayed on First Watch.

The Counselor classification is very political. It often came down to whom you knew, or who knew you. I didn't know anyone. At least no one of consequence that could give me the chance to become a Counselor. So, I languished as an Officer for more years than I should have. Five additional years to be exact, and my position on First Watch was the worst.

One morning, after being relieved of duty, I was walking down the hall in the administration building en route to the staff cafeteria. That was my morning routine. Each morning I would go pick up a pancake breakfast to take home for my daughter before school. I didn't feel like cooking that early in the morning, but I wanted her to have a hot breakfast before she went to school.

As I walked down the hall, I walked past Natalie. I didn't know her but had occasionally seen her around the Institution. I said good morning as I passed her in the hallway. She responded by saying good morning as she continued walking. Suddenly, she came to an abrupt stop.

"Cromwell, she said. Your name is Cromwell?"

"Yes," I responded.

"Is Mother Cromwell, your mother?"

"Yes."

"Is she the church mother at Faith Chapel North?"

"Yes, that's my mom."

"I love her!"

"I do too!" I said, only because I didn't know what else to say.

"Next time you see her, tell her I said hi."

"I sure will," I said, as I turned around and continued walking to the cafeteria. She was still standing there. "Hey, she called after me. Would you like to be a Counselor?" I stopped dead in my tracks. Did I hear her right? I was stunned.

"I would love to," I managed to say.

"Ok, report to my office, in regular clothes on Charlie yard on Thursday." One of the benefits of being a Counselor was you no longer had to wear a uniform. I was getting excited. Today was Tuesday and by Thursday I could have an entirely new career.

"Can I report on Monday? I need to go shopping because I don't have anything to wear." One of the downsides of wearing a uniform all those years is I didn't have any suits or business casual clothes. I had no use for them. By then, uniforms, casual clothes, and club clothes were all I had in my closet.

"Sure. That's fine. That will give me enough time to put in your paperwork. Don't forget to tell your mother I said hi!" She yelled as we both walked away.

I couldn't wait to tell my mother when I got home. I'm sure mom would get a big kick out of it. By being her faithful self, she changed the course of my career. I was giddy. I was almost skipping down the hallway. I couldn't believe it. Five years! I had been trying for five years! And a chance meeting in a hallway, with someone who knew my mother from church, gave me the opportunity I prayed for. Won't He do it!

CHAPTER 10

COUNSELOR

I loved being a Correctional Counselor. I loved everything about it. The autonomy was the best part. Having my own office and no longer having to wear a uniform and boots; being able to work banker's hours with weekends and holidays off, were just a few things. The weekly unit classification committee was a blast! Captain Downing was the best Captain at the Institution, as far as I was concerned. He made every learning experience fun! He seemed to enjoy the lesson more than the outcome. He was a people person, and it showed in everything he did. He clearly enjoyed his job and wanted you to enjoy yours as well. As a result, I looked forward to everything; especially Wednesdays.

Wednesday was committee day each week. He made it a game. If you were late to the committee, you owed him a dollar. That made sure committee always started on time. If you failed to complete your cases promptly, you owed him a dollar. As a result, you always made sure your cases were completed on time. If you didn't know absolutely everything about your case file, when he quizzed you during committee, you owed him a dollar. You were required to pay up, right there, in committee, in front of all your peers. Your peers would talk so much shit when you got something wrong, they could make you feel stupid. In the beginning, there were weeks when I owed the Captain so much that I was afraid to show up to committee. Of course, I kept going anyway. Eventually, the tide turned, and he owed me. He didn't like that part of the game nearly as much. He made sure I knew everything and made me a great Counselor at the same time.

I was a workhorse. I enjoyed the challenge. I worked harder for him than anybody. If you were having a bad day, he would send you home. If it was a non-paid holiday, he would send us home. Captain Downing, the other Counselors, and I became very close working on Charlie yard. Like family, we celebrated birthdays together; occasionally hung out on the weekends, and generally shared our lives: the good and the bad. He invited us to his home, and we got to know his family. It took the sting out of working a Level IV men's prison. Years later, I was incorporating some of his supervisory skills with my subordinates.

The Captain is the highest-ranking uniformed correctional staff on a facility or over a program. They set the tone for the yard. Not just for the inmate population, but staff as well. If the Captain doesn't care about the facility or its people, and rarely comes to his office on the facility, it is reflected in the morale on the yard.

He could raise or lower the morale of the facility just based on his personality and management style. Inmates usually programmed better when they thought they were treated fairly, and their program ran smoothly. Staff liked when the Captain had an open-door policy, and their issues and concerns were considered when considering the policies and procedures of the facility.

The other Captain whose managerial style made being a Counselor interesting, and exciting was Captain Mitchell on Facility B. He and Captain Downing were a lot alike in that regard. He also went the extra mile to make us feel included and needed, instead of like another cog in the wheel. That was quite a feat in state prison. As long as we did our jobs and did them well, he gave us all the autonomy and time off we needed. He wasn't a micro-manager. It wasn't unusual for him to encounter our team walking down the roadway, en route to B yard, pushing our dollies piled high with boxes teaming with central files, to ask us in passing, "What are you guys doing here today? Isn't it a holiday?" What we came to understand that to mean is we could leave for the day if we wanted to. On several occasions, we made a U-turn mid-stride, signed out on the FLSA, and went to a mid-day movie. Those days were our "team-building" days.

It didn't happen often, but small gestures like that were great for morale. It made us feel appreciated for our hard work and like we were truly part of a team. It also made us work harder, because when the Captain asked, "Why are you here today?" You didn't want to be the one Counselor who had to stay behind because you weren't caught up on your caseload.

I appreciated the gesture. Neither Captain mentored me in a traditional sense, but the way they managed their staff gave me an idea of what type of supervisor and eventual manager I wanted to be. It also taught me that the smallest kind gesture could have the biggest impact on people.

Unfortunately, when it was time to bid on our new positions, I didn't have the seniority to stay on either facility. I was moved to a different yard. It wasn't the same anymore. It was no longer quite as fun or enjoyable.

I bounced around to the other facilities for a few years. That allowed me the opportunity to work with every Counselor, for almost every CCII and Captain. I was trained by the best of them. I learned what not to do from the worst of them. I made lifelong friends, and I also met people I hoped to never work with again.

Then I was assigned to Facility D. Occasionally, I would meet up with my old Counselor friends to work in the administration building for the day. It felt good, like old times. We would meet there to work and catch up. We were only required to be on our facilities to conduct interviews with inmates, have office hours, and have a unit classification committee. As long as our casework was complete, and we weren't on any overdue lists we were not heavily supervised. The unwritten rule was not to embarrass the Captain. If you didn't embarrass the Captain, you were all good! I stayed all good. I was a self-starter and needed very little direct supervision. I absolutely loved it.

Then, what we always were afraid of happened. A fellow Counselor was assaulted, in her office, in the housing unit. During an interview with an inmate, she told him he was being transferred. The inmate became enraged. He quickly stood up and punched her in the face. Blood was everywhere. Thank goodness she checked out an alarm that day because sometimes we failed to do so. She pressed her alarm. Before he could attack her further, the cavalry arrived to save her. We always knew we were sitting ducks. We were required to work alone, in our housing unit offices, unlike Officers, who were assigned partners and worked in pairs. Also, the only equipment we were assigned were keys and alarms. We were not required to check out pepper spray or batons, so usually, we didn't.

It turned out that the inmate had mental health issues. After he received a mental health evaluation, he was transferred to Administrative Segregation and given a Rules Violation Report for Assault on a Peace Officer. The assault was unfortunate. The inmate having mental health issues was unfortunate, and unfortunately, the prison population was changing and more and more inmates with mental health issues were being sentenced to state prison every day.

The assault hit me like a ton of bricks. It had a direct impact on me. On all the Counselors. It was shocking. The inmate population usually had somewhat of a hands-off approach to Counselors. We had a great deal of power over their lives. By then, I had worked in prison for more than a decade and during that time, a Counselor had never been assaulted. Being assaulted is always a distinct possibility, but as a Counselor, I felt relatively safe. Now, not so much. The assault heightened my senses and jolted me out of the sense of complacency I had fallen into over the years. One thing I knew for sure, if it happened to her, it could surely happen to me.

After the assault, I began checking out a baton and pepper spray before reporting to the facility. It made me feel safer. The truth had been there along. If an inmate wanted to get you. There wasn't much you could do to avoid it.

As a result of that incident at LAC, the Department updated its "Use of Force" policy. The policy was changed to include the use of any less than lethal item for protection. The new policy change meant if you were under assault, it was recommended that you use anything at your disposal for protection: keys, stapler, the cradle of a telephone, etc. The most important thing was to survive the attack and go home to our family at the end of the day.

TITLE 15, 3268 (6)

Non-Conventional Force

Force that utilizes techniques or instruments that are not specifically authorized in policy, procedures, or training. Depending on the circumstances, non-conventional force can be necessary and reasonable; it can also be unnecessary or excessive.

The prison population was exploding. The Institution was well over capacity, the Department began housing inmates in non-conventional areas, such as housing unit dayrooms and facility gyms. The number of inmates in the housing units increased from 200 to 240. The change also added an additional Floor Officer to the building for added security and to keep the correct Officer/inmate ratio. However, the Correctional Counselor classification was impacted the most. We lost our offices in the housing units. The offices were needed to accommodate medical staff. We were moved to the Education Department, in the facility office area. We called it the bullpen. There was no longer any privacy and even less autonomy. Although our location was changed, for some reason we were never given the keys to unlock the doors. We had to wait for uniformed staff to unlock the door to let us in or out. Let that sink in. If I went to the bullpen alone to work, I would be locked inside the offices with several inmates. There were always too many dangerous blind spots in prisons. But the fact that the Counselors were locked inside the office with inmates, unable to escape if needed, took it to another level.

One of the duties of a CCI was to deliver news to the inmates on our caseloads. Over the years, I delivered more bad news than good. The death of parents, spouses, siblings, and even children. It happened more often than you might think. A large portion of the inmate population was sentenced to life without parole, so they almost always outlived their parents. It was happening far more frequently with the passage of the three-strikes law. Sometimes the inmate was the designated next of kin. As such, he was required to sign the mortuary documents.

Inmate Kenny was on my caseload when his wife died. It was a tragedy. She died from dehydration from botched gastric bypass surgery. For some reason, her death hit me kind of hard. Inmate Kenny was a porter in my housing unit before we relocated to the education area. He often stopped by my office to regale me with stories about his wife and kids. He would tell me how much he loved her and how she was the rock of his family. They had four children, and the kids were her world. I met her once or twice when I stopped by their table in the visiting room. I occasionally stopped in during visits to meet the inmate's families who were on my caseload. Inmate Kenny's wife made an impression on me. I didn't know her, but I knew her more than most. I knew it would be difficult to deliver the bad news. Death was emotional for me. It always had been, but it was my job, so I had to do it.

The Escort Officer brought Inmate Kenny to the facility classification room, locked the door, and went on his way. As the inmate sat down across the table from me I said, "Inmate Kenny, I regret to inform you that your wife passed away," my voice cracked but I continued. "She died as a result of a recent surgery." I blinked back tears as I looked at him.

"What?" He said calmly. "Wow, that's too bad." I understand people handle bad news differently, but he didn't seem fazed at all. I seemed sadder than he did! "Yea, that's too bad." He repeated. His lackluster response made my tears dry quickly. Wow, that was all I could think. I don't think he cared, or at least that is the impression I got.

I stood up so abruptly, I forgot to have him sign the next of kin form until we were standing at the office door. I radioed for the Escort Officer over the institutional radio as I handed him the form to sign. As he reached for the form, he reached past my outstretched hand, grabbed my forearm, and caressed my arm back to my hand as he took the form. I blinked. It took me a minute to figure out what the hell just happened. I hit my alarm and pushed Inmate Kenny against the wall, as I twisted his arm behind his back. Did he just assault me? Really? While I was informing him of his wife's death! The nerve! I probably twisted his arm a little harder than I needed to.

The office door opened as Officers rushed in. They grabbed him. Handcuffed him and escorted him to the Seageant's office. I was still stunned as I retrieved my boxes and went home for the day. Inmate Kenny received a Rules Violation Report (RVR) for Assault on a Peace Officer. He was transferred to Administrative Segregation. Although it should not have been necessary, that incident proved it was a security risk to have the Counselors locked in a work area without a means of escape. The union quickly became involved. The Counselors were assigned the keys we should have had all along.

The Counselor classification was changing so fast it was almost hard for me to keep up. One of the worst changes was our caseloads were no longer assigned by facility and unit, but by central file number. That meant the inmates in my caseload were located all over the Institution, on every yard. That required me to walk to every facility, every day to interview each inmate in my caseload. The bloom was definitely off the rose! The effect on our camaraderie was even worse. We no longer worked together as a team. It devolved into every man for himself. When Counselors usually bided for their position, it was customary to bid for your position as you would have already developed a rapport with the Counselors as well as the inmates on your facility. And you would usually want to continue working for the Captain on your yard. Occasionally, a Counselor would want a change, but that was few and far between. However, with the new change, when the Counselors bided for their positions, the most senior Counselors wouldn't simply bid on their caseloads, which was the fair thing to do. They would bid on the most up-to-date caseload. The caseload that had everything completed with nothing outstanding. My caseload was taken first. One of my peers, who was always on the overdue list and never completed his work on time, took my caseload! He was very arrogant and entitled. I lost respect for many of them and didn't want to work with them anymore. Our morale was at an all-time low, and morale in prison is important. Low morale could be directly correlated to mistakes. In prison, mistakes could be deadly.

The Department of Corrections and Rehabilitation had a big problem due to the exploding prison population. There was a shortage of Correctional Officers to cover the burgeoning population. They couldn't hire and graduate Officers from the Academy fast enough. So, the Department in its infinite wisdom, began the Out-of-Class program. The program allowed correctional staff to work overtime in any position they previously held. Counselors were allowed to work overtime as Officers. Sergeants and Lieutenants could do the same. I was ecstatic. The only thing I missed when I was promoted from Officer to Counselor, was the money. I would have the opportunity to possibly double my income. I was chomping at the bit to get started.

I signed up for the program, and I was one of the first Counselors to put that uniform back on and report for duty. I worked out-of-class every chance I got. Thankfully, when I put the uniform back on, being an Officer was different this time. It was not the same. The level of disrespect I once received from inmates, no longer existed. There was a power shift. I had the power. The power to lock them up. The power to take their jobs. The ultimate power to transfer them to other Institutions where it would be impossible for them to receive visits from their family and friends, and they knew it.

As an Officer, I was fair, firm, and consistent, just like I was taught at the Academy. I always gave an inmate everything he had coming, if not extra when I could. Why did I care? The toilet paper, soap, and tooth powder were not mine. It all belonged to the State. If an inmate needed it, I would give it to him. I didn't power trip. I never used those things to make them grovel. Unlike some Officers, I always treated them like human beings and demanded the same treatment in return. That is how I was raised. I was taught, if you give respect, you get respect in return . . . even in prison. It didn't always work, but most of the time it did.

I liked the new power dynamic. It worked to my advantage. The way I saw it, my overtime shifts should be relatively uneventful, and they usually were.

One Mother's Day, I decided to work overtime. I didn't have anything planned that morning and would see my kid and mom later that day. It was an easy assignment. I was assigned to Facility A, Housing Unit 3

Control Booth. I liked working A yard. It was a Level III yard and almost nothing of any consequence usually happened there. The inmates were less aggressive. Since it was Mother's Day, there was no education, and no program, just the dayroom, and yard. I happily accepted the position and reported to my post.

After reading and signing my post orders, I performed my equipment and weapons check. Then I began running my program. After morning chow was complete, I released the inmates to the yard. For those who didn't want to go to the yard, I released them to the dayroom, turned on the televisions, and began running my shower program. I could complete Correctional Officer duties in my sleep. After being out of uniform for so long, by day two, it all came rushing back as if I never was promoted. The inmates asked for telephone calls, although it wasn't a phone day, I obliged, as it was Mother's Day after all. Anything to make my life easier and my shift pleasant. Besides, the Control Booth could be boring and at least I could listen to inmate phone calls. I swear, sometimes listening to inmate telephone calls was better than watching soap operas. I had a front-row seat to all the begging and pleading as the inmates begged for everything they could get from their families and friends. Begging for visits, shoes, and money, anything they thought was possible was normal. The lies and stories they would tell could be quite entertaining. Some of the phone calls to their mothers and children were heartbreaking. Their mothers were often crying and the children were asking daddy when he would be coming home. No matter how entertaining it could be, I would stay on the lookout for anyone abusing, cursing, or threatening the person on the other line.

Unfortunately, but not surprisingly, I was forced to end one inmates' phone call because he became aggressive and threatening when his mother refused to send him a particular pair of tennis shoes, he requested. No sir, not on my watch, and certainly not on Mother's Day! Not only did I end his phone call, but I also locked him back in his cell for a cooling-off period. It was the end of the dayroom anyway, so it was time to lock up the entire housing unit. That should have been the end of it, but it wasn't.

The inmate was still brooding about me disconnecting his phone call, and whatever residual anger he had for his mother was squarely directed at me. I became the sole focus of his ire.

"Hey, you stupid bitch. Why did you cut off my phone?" he yelled.

I usually didn't respond when an inmate spoke to me that way, but I was bored and I had time that day.

"Who are you talking to?" I inquired over the loudspeaker so the entire housing unit could hear me. I laughed to myself because I knew what was coming.

"You, you stupid bitch!" he said, digging his hole deeper.

The housing unit became deathly quiet. You could hear a pin drop. I didn't have to say anything else. I just sat back and listened.

Another inmate yelled out from behind his cell door. "Hey, dumbass. Don't you know who that is?"

"I don't give a fuck who that dumb bitch is!" the inmate quickly responded. "Who is she?" He inquired with much less fervor.

"That's Cromwell, she's a Counselor. You better watch your mouth." He warned.

"That bitch ain't no Counselor!" he said. His voice was considerably lower this time. Several minutes ticked by.

"Hey, are you a Counselor?" he inquired. I drug it out as long as I could.

"Yes, I am."

I could almost hear the wheels spinning in his head. He was trying to find a way out of his predicament, while still trying to save face in front of the other inmates. Then he gave in and just fell on his sword.

"Hey, Cromwell I'm sorry. I shouldn't haven't have called you a bitch. My bad. I was having a bad day. I didn't know who you were."

"It shouldn't have mattered who I am!"

I released the dayroom and yard. At the end of my shift, once again, I counted my equipment, ensured all weapons and bullets were accounted for, and was relieved of duty. As I walked across the yard, that inmate fell in step beside me. He profusely apologized as we walked across the yard, and I walked out the gate. The power had definitely shifted, and I liked it.

CHAPTER 11

ANATOMY OF A SETUP

Inmate Washer was my clerk. By the time I met him, he had been incarcerated for most of his life. I trusted him more than I did some of the staff. We spent hours and hours together talking about anything and everything while he worked for me. We talked mostly about his life, the prison scuttlebutt, and the general state of prison politics. Inmates generally had a unique perspective on everything.

Most of the time I didn't take them seriously. Their perspectives were, as you could imagine, mostly negative based on their negative life experiences as well as their bad life choices, but not Inmate Washer. Our perspectives were oddly alike. He was intelligent, with an upbeat personality, funny as well, and introspective.

He was one of the only inmates who ever admitted to his crime, and who showed any remorse. While working, we would joke most of the day. It passed the time, and it was a welcomed diversion considering where we were.

I very rarely spoke about my personal life, because at the time, honestly, it wasn't that interesting. He knew the basics. That I was a divorced, single parent, raising my daughter alone. He knew more about my daughter than he probably should have. She was my pride and joy and I spoke about her quite often. It was always a slippery slope how much of my personal life I was willing to share.

People can't understand how easily a bond can form between an inmate and staff. When you spend so much time with them, for weeks, months, and sometimes years you must be very careful not to cross the line. Spending so much time together makes it too easy to share. It is a human connection.

As a Correctional Counselor, my office was in the housing unit. Somedays, I would spend more time with Inmate Washer than I did with my peers. If I had a problem with an inmate in the housing unit, he would handle it for me, and the problem would disappear. On several occasions, he would warn me if something was going down in the housing unit and advise me not to come to the building the next day. Sometimes, I took his advice, sometimes I did not. Most of the time when I didn't take his advice I would regret it. Without fail, there would be some type of incident in the housing unit or on the recreational yard.

It wasn't difficult for me to avoid being overfamiliar with inmates. Bad boys were never my thing. Also, I saw what the inmates did when the lights went out at night. Additionally, there were too many single Correctional Officers available to date. Married ones too, if that was your thing. If you are the type of woman who prefers bad boys, or who are easily manipulated or taken advantage of, working in prison is not for you. Inmates are predators. It is easy for them to identify prey. They seem to know who they can manipulate and push to do things that are against prison policy and the law.

During my career, so many staff, both men and women resigned under investigation or were fired for being overfamiliar with inmates. They were caught bringing in everything from cell phones to drugs. Many female staff, both custodial and non-custodial, lost their jobs for having a personal relationship with an inmate. Sometimes there would be weeks of someone being walked off daily. The institutional rumor mill would generally proceed each dismissal. It would be the hot topic of the day. We would talk about what we knew or thought we knew. What we suspected and did not suspect. The conversation du jour was how they got caught. Then it would die down. Only to have it happen again and again.

To me, an inmate was a means to an end. They were the way I supported myself and my family. I quietly despised inmates. They always reminded me of the type of men I was exposed to growing up on the wrong side of the tracks in Los Angeles. Negative men who were users and predators, always looking for a mark. I was never tempted to cross the line.

The more time Inmate Washer and I spent together, the closer we became. I began looking forward to seeing him every day. As my clerk, he had many duties. The most important one was to control the other inmate's access to me in the housing unit. He kept my schedule. If an inmate didn't show up for his appointment, he would quickly locate the inmate and ensure he made his scheduled appointment. I didn't know how he did it. Honestly, I did not care. I was required to take a certain number of inmates to unit classification committee weekly to ensure I was in compliance with my caseload. Inmate Washer was my secret weapon to ensure I was always in compliance.

He was very protective of me. He sat his desk outside my office door. No one came within an inch of my office without an appointment or unless I called for them. He was my bodyguard. He protected me, not only from the inmates in the building but from the inmates on the yard. If anything happened, they would have to go through him to get to me. Knowing this gave me a certain level of comfort.

I had experienced that protection before. There seemed to always be a level of ownership the inmates felt for the female staff they directly worked for. Whether in the housing unit, on the yard, or in the classrooms. Most of the time, if you were fair, firm, and gave the inmates what they had coming, they would be respectful, appreciative, and do everything in their power to be helpful. Of course, that wasn't always the case for all inmates. But for many, you became a de facto big sister, auntie, or mother figure. You just had to be cautious and aware of the ones who were manipulative.

As Inmate Washer's direct Supervisor, I dictated his job duties. He did everything from cleaning my office, corralling the inmates for their appointments, to moving my boxed central files from my dolly and placing them in my office. Eventually, I directed him to meet me at the facility gate each morning to push my dolly across the yard to my office. While walking to the building we would discuss my schedule for the day and his daily assignments. That is when the trouble started.

The Officers on the yard became suspicious of our relationship. I began hearing rumors that I was being overfamiliar with Inmate Washer. That I had somehow crossed the line. The biggest mistake I made was trying to ignore the rumors instead of confronting them head-on. The biggest issue seemed to be that Inmate Washer was awaiting my arrival every morning at the facility gate and would "escort" me to the housing unit while pushing my dolly. What the Officers failed to consider is, as my assigned clerk, I determined his job duties. I was subject to zero disrespect from other inmates if he was walking with me to the housing unit. It was definitely a strategy. Usually, when I walked across the yard alone, inmates would rush up to me with some nonsense or other. It was annoying as well as dangerous.

They didn't want to understand. I am sure it was much more entertaining to think the worst. Eventually, it all came to a head. One morning as Inmate Washer and I were walking from the gate to the building a random Yard Officer said, loud enough for everyone to hear,

"There goes the Counselor with her inmate boyfriend!" I stopped dead in my tracks. I confronted the Officer and dared him to repeat what he said. Of course, he would not. I made sure every Officer and inmate in the vicinity who heard what he said, also heard my response. "Listen you asshole, Inmate Washer is my clerk. I decide what his duties are. I directed him to meet me at the facility gate every morning to push my heavy ass dolly. His job description states, and other duties as assigned. If you don't like him pushing my dolly, then you can show up every morning and push it yourself. If not, shut the fuck up!" He didn't respond. I'd made my point. We continued to the housing unit. That should have been the end of it.

After the run-in with the Officer on the yard. I thought any talk or innuendo of overfamiliarity was over. I was wrong. A few days later, when I arrived at work, Inmate Washer informed me that the day before, after I left the building for the day, the Control Booth Officer had called him my boyfriend. I thought about it for a while and concluded that I would once again, address the issue head-on with that Officer.

He was the Third Watch Control Booth Officer, which meant he would not be in until 2:00 p.m. that day. I stewed all day waiting for Third Watch. Once the Control Booth Officer arrived and settled in for the day, I requested he let me into his Control Booth. Once there, I let him have it!

"I understand yesterday you called Inmate Washer my boyfriend in front of the entire housing unit," It took everything in me to remain calm and to keep my voice on an even keel. It was a rhetorical question, as I did not wait for him to answer.

"Don't you ever, even in jest, say something like that about an inmate and a female staff member! You can ruin someone's career, by making unproven allegations. You also leave yourself open to a slander and defamation lawsuit. If I ever hear you say something like that about me, not only will I file a complaint, I will sue you, and you can explain yourself to the Custody Captain as well as a judge. With that, I left the control booth, walked across the yard, and filed a complaint with the Union President. I wouldn't stand for my character being maligned, or the possibility of my career being jeopardized, and possibly being under investigation for something I didn't do. I had been through that before. I was not going through it again.

I am not sure what became of my complaint, but I certainly put everyone on notice. I was not to be played with. Everything died down after that. I didn't hear any more rumors and no one dared to say anything else again. At least not to my face.

Several months later, I arrived at work as usual. Inmate Washer was not at the facility gate. He had never missed a day since I made that one of his assigned duties. I had to admit, I was a little pissed, as I didn't like pushing my dolly across the yard by myself.

When I arrived in the building he came into my office. Right away I could tell something was wrong. Something was out of the ordinary. Inmate Washer was always suited and booted. He was meticulous about his appearance. His blue chambray shirt was always ironed, and his blue jeans were always starched. He was old school and everything he wore had creases. His state-issued boots were always so shined, you could see yourself in them. He always took pride in his appearance as well as his job. Today, for some reason he was off. He was disheveled. I could tell he had not done his hygiene; his hair was not combed, and his face was not washed. He looked dirty. If I had gotten close enough, I'm sure he smelled bad.

"What's wrong with you?" I asked.

"Nothing," he replied.

He spoke in one-word sentences with no elaboration and his affect was flat. This was not the same person I knew. I was a little worried as I had seen this before. Sometimes, when an inmate received bad news, a Dear John letter, or even a negative response from the parole board their demeanor could change, and they sometimes took it out on the staff. He sat down in the chair across from my desk. I had already decided to send him home for the rest of the day, to give him some time to pull himself together. I popped a stick of gum in my mouth and took a deep breath. What happened next would forever change how I interacted with inmates for the remainder of my career.

"Give me a piece of gum," he said.

My eyes narrowed. "What did you say?" I asked as I looked him directly in his eyes. I heard him clearly the first time and was praying he wouldn't say it again.

"Give me a piece of gum," he repeated.

"When have I ever given you a piece of gum?" I was still hoping he would laugh it off as if it was a joke, so I could give him a pass for having a bad day and I would not have to do what I was hoping I would not have to do.

"You've done it before." I could feel the heat rising up my collar to my face. I am sure my eyes were red as well.

I had been working in prison for over a decade by then. Of course, I had experienced this before. I knew what was happening. We received training for this exact scenario; first in the Academy and several times throughout the years in Institutional Service Training. Yes, I knew exactly what was happening. However, I was confused as to why Inmate Washer was doing it. I stood up so forcefully, my chair crashed to the ground. I looked him directly in his face and shouted, "Not only have I never given you a piece of gum, you asshole! But I've also never given you anything! Get the hell out of my office!" I screamed. "And don't you come back, unless I send for you!" What the hell just happened? I was so shaken up that I packed my boxes, left the Institution, and went home for the rest of the day.

A few years earlier, when I was a brand-new Officer, a friendly housing unit porter began trying to get close to me. I would find cards and letters left for me in our housing unit office. He was cool. I liked him. He was a good porter and had the gift of gab. We would chit-chat as we went about the business of running the building. He was always cheerful and did a great job. Eventually, he crossed the line. One day when I returned to work from my regular days off. He met me at the podium.

"Cromwell, I missed you while you were gone," he said.

"Really?" I replied.

"Yes. I just really like talking to you. You remind me of my sister. Because I miss you so much, would you mind if I wrote to you on your days off?"

"How do you miss me so much in two days? And what do we have to talk about that can't wait until I return to work?"

That should have given him an indication that he was crossing the line. He refused to take the hint.

"I don't know, I like you and just miss you when you're not here." Now I was mad.

"If you like me so much, then why are you trying to make me lose my job?" He began trying to backpedal.

"I didn't mean it like that," he stuttered.

"Well, how did you mean it then? You know it's illegal for staff to correspond with inmates! You like me so much, but you don't care if I lose my job?"

I fired him on the spot. I had him immediately transferred to another yard. He thought he could manipulate me. I don't know what had given him that impression, but he found out how wrong he was.

Inmates had 365 days to focus on us; to find any little thing they think they can use to manipulate us. It is insidious and before you know it you have fallen into their trap. When they target you, they usually start small by being friendly, jovial, and very complimentary. If they work for you, they make sure they do the best job they can while putting you at ease in their presence. They want you to think they are different from any other inmate you have ever met. Lulling you into a false sense of security and pushing you to lower your guard. They attempt to get you to do something small, something seemingly innocuous that you know you're not supposed to do, just this one time, just for him. Nobody will ever know. It will be just between you and him. Then later he will use that one little thing against you. Before you know it you are bringing in drugs or sucking his dick. He owns you at that point. You are caught up. There's nowhere to go but down and there is no way out. If you are smart, you will resign while under investigation.

Otherwise, one day you will find yourself being handcuffed and escorted to the gate. Your picture will be plastered all over the Institution on a memo that reads: "If this person attempts to enter the Institution, please dial 211." You lose your job, your friends, and sometimes even your family.

It is not only against prison policy, but it is against the law to have a sexual relationship with an inmate. Inmates are wards of the State, and as such cannot give consent. Staff is always in a position of authority, and it is an abuse of their power. Not only are they jeopardizing their safety and the safety and security of the Institution, but they are jeopardizing their freedom as well.

The setup happens in every jail and prison. In every state and territory. Anytime someone has control over someone else, you can believe someone is abusing their power, and someone is falling for the setup.

I thought about the incident with Inmate Washer for the rest of the day. What I could not figure out is why it happened. I knew what it was and that it was a textbook setup. I was convinced that whoever was behind it was listening to our conversation. My office was either bugged, or a camera was surreptitiously placed there during off-hours. Or they were listening to our conversation via the intercom system. Every office inside the institutional housing unit has an intercom. The intercom is in the Control Booth. Its purpose is to be able to easily relay information from the Control Booth Officer to either the Correctional Officer or the Counselor. Sometimes the intercom is the last line of defense if there is trouble, and you can't use the telephone or the radio. Anyone in the Control Booth could use the intercom to listen to our conversation. I just didn't know why anyone would want to.

The next day, Inmate Washer failed to meet me at the gate again. I knew why this time. Before coming to work that morning, I already decided to fire him and transfer him to another facility. I quickly found out I would not have to. When I requested the Control Booth Officer release him from his cell and send him to my office, he told me Inmate Washer had been "rolled up" by the Security Squad the night before.

I called the Security Squad to find out what happened. Two days before, based on confidential information obtained by a prison informant, a search was conducted on his cell. A large number of drugs and cell phones were found.

Suddenly, everything made sense. Inmate Washer attempted to set me up in exchange for either a reduced sentence or not being charged with drug and cell phone possession. Each offense was a felony and carried a lengthy sentence in Administrative Segregation. He was immediately transferred to Pelican Bay State Prison.

I never found out what he told the Squad, or what they promised him, if anything, but what he attempted to do to me was classic. I would have loved to know where the setup originated. Was it Inmate Washer who thought he could use me as a bargaining chip? Or was the Security Squad investigating me because of the institutional rumor about me having an illicit relationship with an inmate? I do not know. What I did know was, had I fallen for the okie dokie, my career would have been over. So much for thinking an inmate could have your back. As I looked back over our relationship. Every encounter looked different. Was every conversation, every exchange, every laugh, simply his way of lulling me into a false sense of security? His attempt to get me to lower my guard, so he could use it to his advantage later. It would have been so easy to absentmindedly hand him a piece of gum. I was convinced the previous encounter with my porter all those years before kept me a little more guarded than I would have naturally been.

Unknowingly, that one incident along with my training had prepared me for the setup.

I swore I would never put myself in that position again. My heart hardened. When I went to work from then on, my armor and shield were firmly in place. After all, inmates were just a means to an end; a way I had chosen to support my family.

TO LIVE AND DIE IN LA

As a female living in Los Angeles County, working in its only prison at times could be precarious. Inmate families sometimes moved to the Antelope Valley to be closer to their incarcerated loved ones to visit more frequently. So once the inmate was paroled, he would usually stay in the city, instead of returning to where he lived before he was incarcerated. Occasionally, I ran into a parolee while running errands on my day off.

Once, while out and about, I stopped into the local Pep Boys to purchase a new battery for my car. As I moved through the aisles, I noticed a good-looking young man moving in unison with me. When I moved, he moved. When I stopped, he stopped. Whatever aisle I went down, so did he. He was making me nervous. He was careful to maintain a little distance. He looked vaguely familiar. It threw me off as I racked my brain, trying to pinpoint where I had seen him before. No matter how hard I tried I could not place him. Then a light bulb went off. I decided to confront him. I slowly walked up to him. He smiled. I breathed a sigh of relief.

"What yard do I know you from?" I asked.

"Minimum." He said.

"How long have you been out?" I asked as my heart raced.

"Two months."

"How are you doing?" I asked as nonchalantly as I could.

"I'm doing well."

"I'm glad. You stay out, okay?" I said as I walked away.

"I will." He responded as he stood there looking at me.

I left the store without purchasing anything. I was okay. That was all that mattered. I could purchase that item another day.

On a different occasion, while walking through a mall in L.A. with my family, I found myself being picked up and spun around. When I was put down, I was staring in the face of one of my porters from C yard. It is a very small world. He was happier to see me than I was to see him. Of course, he didn't know that. I'm sure if you walked past us at that moment, we would have looked like old friends greeting one another. We stood there for a few minutes and caught up. Then went our separate ways.

In those situations, I wouldn't say I was afraid, but I would be lying if I wasn't concerned. I was glad that I always treated inmates like human beings. If I behaved like some of my peers, those encounters could have turned out very differently. I am glad I had home training. I was taught to always treat people the way you want to be treated, even in prison, because it's simply the right thing to do.

For my single sisters, the situation was even more dangerous. A few years before, a female Officer was fired. She unwittingly dated an inmate on parole. She was a Correctional Officer for eight years when her boyfriend of a year was pulled over during a routine traffic stop. He was driving her car. When the license plate was checked, the car was registered to her. Just like that, her career was over, and she was back in the hustle, the struggle, and the grind. She said she didn't know. Of course, many didn't believe her, but I did. Honestly, how were we to know? We couldn't run a background check on anyone.

I developed an entire speech when I was dating, for just that purpose. I was often accused of using an application from the men I dated. I always asked the following questions, Are you now or have you ever been in jail, prison, or on probation or parole? Although I felt I was doing my due diligence, people lie. If I met someone at a restaurant, nightclub, or anywhere in public, how would I know if they were on parole? It is unfortunate, but that is the gamble we took when we chose to work at a prison and live in the same city. However, my encounter with my porter in the mall in Los Angeles was proof that we were never really safe anywhere.

CHAPTER 12

RIOT ON THE YARD

For several months I enjoyed working overtime. The money was great. The respect from the inmates was even better. No more being yelled at, cursed out, and called names. I had entered, what I liked to call, the golden age of my career. I was a Correctional Counselor and could also work overtime. The best of both worlds. This was the first time that was an option since I had joined the Department of Corrections and Rehabilitation.

Although we garnered a certain level of respect from the inmate population, the correctional staff was a horse of a different color. They didn't think Counselors should be allowed to work overtime. The reason we were allowed to work out-of-class in the first place was to support them. There were not enough Correctional Officers to cover all the positions in the Institution. If we weren't allowed to pick up the slack, the Officers would have been ordered over.

Excessive order overs overwork staff and lowers morale. As a result, Officers call in sick more. It is a vicious cycle. The Officers should have been grateful, but they weren't. Instead, they were jealous. Everything in an Institution is a competition. Who has the biggest house? Who has the best car? Who worked the most overtime? Who earned the most money? Once, while hosting a training conference at the Institution, the Warden was asked if there were any dignitaries from headquarters in attendance based on the type of cars in the parking lot.

There wasn't. The Jaguars, Mercedes Benz, Corvettes, Lexus' and Escalades belonged to the Correctional Officers at the Institution.

Every year the Sacramento Bee published an article that listed the highest-paid state workers. Each year, many correctional staff made the list. Keeping up with the Jones' was alive and well at LAC. I didn't care about any of that. I just wanted to work.

One day I received a call from the Watch Office. They offered me Facility B, Housing Unit 1 for overtime. I happily accepted it. Facility B was a Level III yard and usually ran well, without too many issues. The Level III yards were not quite as violent as the Level IV yards. The inmates had fewer points and as a result, usually had a release date. Most of them did not want to mess up and add time to their sentence. Since it was my day off, I quickly put on my uniform and headed to work. When I assumed my post, I read and signed my post orders as usual. I counted my equipment and began running my program. I released the yard and the dayroom. I ran the shower program along with the telephones. Just another day at the office.

About an hour or so into my shift everything changed. I happened to be standing at the back window watching the recreational yard. The yard was running as it generally did. Inmates sitting at the tables and benches. Inmates exercising.

Inmates playing handball and basketball. The Officers were milling about the yard. It was nothing unusual. Suddenly, a fistfight broke out in front of work change. The yard gun did what he was required to do. He pushed the yard alarm and began yelling "Get down, get down, get down!" He put the yard down. All uninvolved inmates quickly sat down on the yard. I just as quickly rushed to the control panel, ensured the inmates in the dayroom got down and opened both rotunda doors so the housing unit Officers could respond to the yard. I grabbed my weapon and returned to the back window to keep an eye on the yard.

Just as the Officers were quelling the disturbance, in unison, the Hispanic inmates stood up and began attacking the Black inmates. It looked like a wave. It was surreal. The Hispanic inmates punched, kicked, and stabbed any Black inmate within reach. The Black inmates were severely outnumbered and caught off guard. It was a riot! It was a massacre! It seemed like hours. Correctional Officers began pouring into the facility as the riot continued.

The gunner fired again, and again, and again. Several Control Booth Officers fired their weapons as well. Lethal and less-than-lethal munitions were rapidly deployed, but the riot continued. Boom! Boom! Boom! Shots continued to ring out from everywhere. It was almost melodic. It was all you could hear, even as the gunner continued to yell for the inmates to get down. Plumes of smoke bellowed over the entire yard as the Officers advanced utilizing pepper spray, trying to quell the disturbance. Finally, the inmates began getting down. What felt like hours, had transpired in mere minutes.

When it was over, the Black inmates lay injured and bleeding. Several were medevacked to surrounding hospitals and rushed into surgery. Officers were deployed to the rooftops as Correctional Counselors joined in to help handcuff and escort the inmates, as the Control Booth Officers locked up our respective buildings.

The cleanup took hours. There wasn't enough equipment or staff to complete the mission. The Institution was locked down and all staff were redirected to Bravo yard to help with the cleanup and after action.

We worked late into the night to get the Black inmates' medical treatment, and to generate Rules Violation Reports (RVR) for the

Hispanic inmates. Since there wasn't enough room to re-house them all in the Administrative Segregation units, a makeshift unit was created on the facility. Only after all involved staff completed their written reports were we allowed to go home. By then, it was into the wee hours of the morning. It was a long, long day. There is an expression in CDCR, "All money, ain't good money!" Man, did that prove true that day.

The ensuing investigation uncovered that morning, the Hispanic inmates called mandatory yard. Mandatory yard is when the shot caller commands his population not to go to program, i.e., education, work, appointments, or vocations, but to report to the recreational yard instead. If any inmate failed to follow directions, he would have a green light put on him.

The day before the riot, the Hispanic inmates hid their weapons on the yard. The Black inmates tried to fight back, but the Hispanic inmates had inmate-manufactured stabbing devices (shanks). They planned to cause a distraction (the fistfight in front of work change) and attack the Black inmates when the yard went down. They had specific directions to kill as many Black inmates as possible.

The premeditated attack was due to unpaid drug debts, as well as the Hispanic inmates, feeling disrespected by the Blacks. The Black inmates were livid, and not just at the Hispanic inmates. They were also angry at the Correctional Officers.

They thought the Officers set them up. The Officers should have noticed and reported when no Hispanic inmates showed up to program that morning.

There were rumors that the Black inmates declared open season on all Correctional Officers. A thorough threat assessment was conducted to ensure there was no viable threat against staff. It was determined that the Black inmates started the rumor in an attempt to save face. Nothing ever became of the rumor or the threat. As a result of that horrific riot, CDCR once again updated its policy. If an inmate failed to report to education, work, or vocation within fifteen minutes of his designated start time, the Officer is required to contact the housing unit to locate the inmate. If the inmate cannot be located, the Yard Sergeant will put the yard down and locate the inmate. If the inmate still cannot be located, the yard will be recalled until the inmate can be found, only then will the recreational yard resume. The new policy was an attempt to ensure what transpired on Facility B would never happen again.

The Out-Of-Class program continued and ran as intended for the most part. However, there was a Watch Sergeant who had a negative opinion about Correctional Counselors working out-of-class as Officers. The Correctional Officers could only complain. The Watch Sergeant could do something about it.

The way the program worked, if a Counselor wanted to work overtime that day, we would sign up on the voluntary overtime sheet located at the front sally port. You could call in and request the sally port Officer place you on the list, but it was better to sign up yourself to avoid any issues. The Counselors and Officers had separate sign-up sheets. The Search and Escort Officers picked up the sign-up sheets at a designated time and delivered them to the Watch Sergeant. Once he received the sign-up sheets he would begin hiring for overtime based on seniority. The staff with the highest seniority would be called first, so on and so forth, down the list, until all vacant positions were covered. It was simple enough. However, every time a certain Sergeant worked in the Watch Office, the Counselor's overtime sheet would mysteriously disappear and somehow not make it to the watch. Therefore, regardless of your seniority, you wouldn't be offered any overtime that day. I began keeping track of when I would not get offered overtime and correlating it with when that Sergeant was on duty.

After not receiving any offers of overtime for a few days, I went to the Watch Office to confront the Sergeant over the "missing" sign-up sheets.

He was unwilling to discuss the issue. Instead, he became enraged and profane, but I stood my ground!

"I know you're throwing away our sign-up sheets," I said.

"Prove it!" He challenged. He began yelling and screaming at me to get out of his office.

"Don't you mean the State's office?" I yelled, as I turned on my heels and stormed out of the office. The nerve! The unmitigated gall! All he had done was piss me off. He wanted me to prove it. That is exactly what I intended to do. Upon storming out of the Watch Office, I found the Union President and promptly filed a complaint against the Sergeant as well as the Institution. I refused to allow him or anyone else to disrespect me or push me around. Especially when I had proof, and he was wrong. While in the Academy, we were often warned that the problems we would encounter in the Institution would mostly be because of staff and not inmates. That was certainly proving true.

The complaint was a long and tedious process. I was convinced it was designed to wear you down, so you might eventually give up and drop it, but they didn't know me. When something was stuck in my craw, I was like a bulldog that wouldn't let it go. The entire process took almost an entire year to complete. The Watch Office continually threw up roadblocks. They were censured by the judge on several occasions for not providing the documentation ordered. I was not deterred. For me, it was a matter of principle at that point. We were assigned to arbitration.

During the arbitration hearing, the Institution was ill-prepared. They had no proof. They called no witnesses but had plenty of excuses. While I was fully prepared with documentation, witnesses, and a timeline of what had occurred only when the Sergeant was on duty. I had my ducks in a row. The judge saw through all their excuses. I eventually prevailed. I settled out of court for an undisclosed amount. What that showed me was, never let anyone push you around. As my dear mother would say, "Right always wins in the end."

When I won my case, my fellow Counselors thought it should have been a class-action lawsuit. It wasn't. Nobody was interested in helping me. No one assisted in filing the complaint or obtaining any of the needed documentation. They certainly were not interested in going to arbitration with me. In fact, most of them thought I should have never filed a complaint in the first place. They were afraid that I was rocking the boat. Once I won the case and was awarded the settlement everyone wanted a piece. It was typical. They were not interested in doing the work, but they were interested in reaping the rewards.

Unfortunately, the Out-Of-Class program was poorly planned and poorly executed. It was only a stopgap; meant to fill vacant positions in the meantime, while the Department pushed hard to hire more Officers and get them through the Academy. I am not sure if it was intended to be the answer indefinitely, but it seemed to be doomed to fail from the start. Human Resources weren't appropriately trained before the beginning of the program. They never really seemed to understand how to execute it. I was convinced my overtime check was never calculated correctly. Each month, when I would ask how my pay was calculated, I was usually met with hostility. Nobody could fully explain the unnecessarily complicated formula or how we were paid. I knew we were assigned two pay numbers. My regular pay was calculated as a Counselor and my overtime pay was supposed to be calculated at the Officer's pay rate. It never seemed to add up correctly.

At some point, either the Department did not need the program anymore, or it became too complicated to maintain. If I had filed a grievance at LAC, how many others had done so at other Institutions? The program was eventually canceled. Counselors were disappointed, as was I. The difference is, they blamed me.

Some of them thought my grievance had precipitated the cancellation of the program. I am not sure if it did or not. And I really didn't care. I just knew what the Sergeant did was wrong, and I had an obligation to ensure he did not continue doing it.

By then, I was a Counselor for six years and had been in the Department for thirteen. I felt I had obtained all the knowledge I could from the Counselor classification, coupled with no longer being able to work overtime, I was ready for a career change. I wanted to learn more, do more, earn more and this was no longer the way to do it. I was used to the additional money and it was hard to give it up this time. I also wanted a greater level of responsibility.

Luckily for me, that was the year of promotional examinations. The Department usually offered promotional examinations every 2-4 years, depending on its need. I took every test I qualified for and awaited the results. To my surprise, I was very competitive in the Correctional Lieutenants Examination. I was shocked. I was not expecting that. I thought I would promote to Correctional Counselor II. I never genuinely considered being a Lieutenant. I wasn't sure I ever wanted to go back to wearing a uniform every day. I wasn't sure I ever wanted to do shift work or work weekends again, but now, I was considering it all. I had to quickly decide because the Lieutenant interviews were approaching fast. I decided to ask my friend Daniel for advice.

Daniel and I had become friends over the years. He was the Lieutenant on Facility B when I was the Counselor assigned to the yard. He was loud, boisterous, and commanded any space he was in. You could easily identify him coming down the hall because he wore taps on the bottom of his shoes. His office was in the front hall, just as you entered the building. I passed it every morning en route to the Counselor's office. One day, I had an extra coffee, stopped in to chat and that became our daily routine. Some mornings I would bring breakfast or a snack.

Depending on what was on the agenda for the day, we could talk for hours. He was the number one Lieutenant in the Institution as he had been a Lieutenant the longest and had the best seniority. When I told Daniel I was considering becoming a Lieutenant he said, "Baby, I know I make this look easy, but everybody can't do this job!" Ain't that nothing! I was perturbed and disappointed. Lesson learned. Be careful whose advice you seek. That was the last time I would ask his opinion about anything concerning my career.

I decided it wouldn't hurt to interview for the position. I could consider it right up until the time I was offered the job. If, I was offered the job.

The day of the Lieutenant interviews finally arrived. I wore my favorite blue suit. I was hoping it would bring me good luck. For some reason I was nervous. I had not interviewed for a job in years. I didn't know what to expect or what would be required. I was as prepared as I could be. I was hoping for the best. I didn't tell anybody that I was interviewing for the position. In case it didn't go well, no one would know, and I wouldn't have egg on my face.

I sat in the lobby of the administration building where the interviews were being held and waited for my name to be called. As I was patiently waiting, several of my peers, friends, and Supervisors stopped to ask me why I was sitting in the lobby that morning. I made up different excuses, depending on who was asking the question. I just wasn't ready for anyone to know. I still had not made up my mind if I wanted the position. I knew that once the information hit the yards all kinds of bullshit would be coming my way. What I was possibly doing, had never been done before. To my knowledge, nobody at LAC had ever been promoted from Correctional Counselor to Correctional Lieutenant. It simply was not done. It was not the correct order of things.

As a Correctional Officer, the way you are promoted up the chain of command is: Sergeant, Lieutenant, Captain, Associate Warden, Chief

Deputy Warden, and then finally Warden. As a Correctional Counselor, your promotional pattern is: Correctional Counselor I, Correctional Counselor II, Correctional Counselor III, then Associate Warden, Chief Deputy Warden, then Warden. What you did not do is promote from Counselor to Lieutenant without any direct supervisory experience. It was rare, but I had finally made up my mind that was exactly what I was going to do. If the California Department of Corrections and Rehabilitation said it could be done, who was going to tell me I couldn't? Oh, they could make it hard for me, but they couldn't stop me. Just let them try. They wouldn't win, because by then, I was intent on blazing a trail!

Very few people would understand why I was back in uniform. Why I wanted to go back to shift work and working weekends. They did not have to understand. I did. I nervously sat in that lobby for hours, until my name was finally called. Less than an hour later, I was no longer a Correctional Counselor. I was a newly promoted Correctional Lieutenant at CSP-LAC.

CHAPTER 13

PRISON GANGS

A prison gang is an inmate organization that operates within the prison system. It has a corporate entity, exists into perpetuity, and whose membership is restrictive, mutually exclusive, and requires a lifetime commitment.

As long as there have been prisons, there have been prison gangs. Prison gangs were originally formed for protection. Inmates from the same street gangs and neighborhoods formed prison gangs to protect themselves from their rivals while incarcerated. Their rivals were housed in the same facilities and prison yards.

However, it did not take long for them to start vying for control and to begin engaging in the same illegal activities they participated in while on the street, i.e. drugs, prostitution, and weapons. At least half the prison population is convicted of at least one violent crime. So, it is natural or second nature for gangs to use violence and intimidation to control the prison population.

Prison gangs exploded in the California prison system in the 1980s with the influx of crack in neighborhoods, the large-scale arrest and conviction of street gang members, as well as the mass incarceration of the populace. California locks up a large percentage of its citizens. Therefore, it has more prison gangs than any other state.

Race, ethnicity, street gang affiliation, and geographical location are the determining factors in prison gangs, unlike street gangs which are generally formed by neighborhoods and due to proximity.

A prison gang is also a criminal enterprise. They are the principal source of discord and disorder within the prison system. They control all criminal activities inside prison walls.

In addition to controlling the criminal activities, they decide who can and cannot live in the facilities and the housing units. In prison, there is a code of honor. As well as a hierarchy. Rapists and child molesters are at the bottom of the hierarchy and generally looked down upon, so their movement and where they can live are severely limited. When an inmate moves onto the yard, the inmate is "required" to show his papers. The required paperwork indicates what the inmate is convicted of. It will be determined whether he is approved to be housed there. If an inmate refuses to provide the information he must get off the yard as soon as possible before he has a green light on him. In response to this problem, California developed the Sensitive Needs Yard (SNY). The Sensitive Needs Yard houses gang dropouts, inmates convicted of sex crimes, as well as other inmates who cannot safely house on the facilities.

Violence and intimidation are used to control gang members. If a gang member is given an order to assault someone, there is no disagreeing or opting out. If he fails to follow directions he will be assaulted, and dropping out is not an option.

Street gang members can drop out by moving to another neighborhood, city, or state, but prison gang members don't have that luxury. They can request a move to Administrative Segregation, but there is no guarantee they will be safe even there.

To compete for control of the yard, gang members need numbers. The obvious optics of the yard usually allow for easy identification of which race is in control of what yard.

In 1994, when I joined the Department, Black inmates vastly outnumbered all races in the California prison system. Primarily due to the mass incarceration of Black men, the criminalization of crack addiction, and eventually the Crime Bill and the three-strikes law. So, due to their sheer numbers, the Black inmates controlled the yards. Over time, due to migration, illegal immigration, and the growth of Hispanic street gangs, Hispanics began to outnumber the Blacks in the California prison system and a power shift took place.

In Los Angeles County, Hispanics are the largest demographic. They are 48% of the population, while African Americans make up just 9%. Blacks are overrepresented in the State prison system for sure, but as long as LAC has more Hispanic inmates than any other race, the Hispanics will control the prison.

The primary prison gangs in the California prison system are:

The Black Guerrilla Family, which was founded in the 1960s by a former Black Panther.

The Mexican Mafia, started in 1957 in DVI.

Nuestra Familia, started in the 1960s in Soledad Prison.

The Surenos started in the 1960s. They are American-raised Hispanics from Southern California who has ties to the Mexican Mafia.

The Nortenos, started in the 1960s. They are America-raised Hispanics of Northern California who originally had ties to the Mexican Mafia, but broke off into their faction when they felt they were not treated fairly in prison. It is uncommon to find a Norteno housed in a Southern California prison. If so, they are single-celled, quickly classified, and expeditiously transferred up north for their protection. They are not allowed to walk the general population yard for fear of being stabbed or killed.

The Aryan Brotherhood (AB) was founded in the 1960s in San Quentin State Prison.

Although prison gangs are problematic, street gangs are the main problem. As LAC is Los Angeles County's only state prison, the Hispanic street gangs, Bloods, Crips, and Nazi lowriders and their sub-sets cause the majority of issues in the daily operation of the Institution. When two or more factions of the same gang have issues, it is difficult to identify the culprits because they are of the same race, the same ethnicity, and can be from the same neighborhoods. It wasn't unusual to have a sub-set of a street gang on a modified program, or lockdown at any given time.

Usually, there is an uneasy truce between the gangs on the yard. They superficially get along because it behooves them to do so. Sometimes, they even work together for a common goal. But that is rare. They segregate themselves from each other to avoid conflict as much as possible. It is highly uncommon to see inmates of different races living together, although nothing precludes them from doing so. They self-segregate, as The California Department of Corrections and Rehabilitation has a policy against segregation.

The Hispanic gangs are very disciplined. They work together as a unit. They regularly call mandatory yard to maintain a tight grip on their members. Most mornings you will find them on the handball court working out. As staying in shape is an important tenet of their organization. You can hear the leader calling cadence while the members complete burpees, jumping jacks, push-ups, and sit-ups. Their mission is to always be ready for whatever happens.

Each Institution has a gang unit. Their chief mission is to identify and validate gang members, to intercept their correspondence, document their methods of communication, and interrupt their criminal activities. Doing nothing is not an option, because doing so allows the problems to fester and grow. A prison is already a dangerous place for inmates and staff alike. So, allowing unchecked gang activity makes it even more dangerous.

Every major incident or disturbance I witnessed during my career was primarily or partially due to gang activity.

CHAPTER 14

BACK ON THE BLOCK

It was Memorial Day weekend when I was promoted to Lieutenant. The information spread through the Institution like wildfire. As usual, everyone seemed to have an opinion about my promotion and most of it was negative. As I didn't have an assignment yet, I was required to report to the Institution to obtain one. Once there, I went to the Watch Office to talk to the Custody Captain to find out my first assignment. I heard through the grapevine that the Custody Captain was so disturbed by my promotion, he pulled the hiring package to see if I was truly competitive or if my promotion was a "homie hookup." The Chief Deputy Warden and I were friends. We attended the same high school. He must have been sorely disappointed to find out I ranked number one in the interview.

I stepped into the sally port that day in my uniform with my shiny new Lieutenant bars firmly attached to my collar. All conversations stopped. You could hear a pin drop. Several people looked over their shoulders directly at me but didn't say anything. It is as if it needed to sink in. They began whispering amongst themselves, then someone, I'm not entirely sure said, "Hey Cromwell, are you acting?"

"Nope," I replied. There was a Lieutenant in the sally port who I had known since I was an Officer. He looked me square in the eye. I smiled. He didn't and turned his head. So, that's how it's going to be? I thought to myself. The look he gave me was a sign of things to come. He couldn't get out of that sally port fast enough to alert his peers that I had arrived. I stepped through the sally port and began walking to Central Operations to get my first assignment.

When I arrived, the Custody Captain was not in his office. However, the job changes were already posted on the board. Effective Sunday night, I was assigned to First Watch.

As punishment for promoting to Lieutenant, I was assigned to First Watch, I should say. I could hardly believe it. I had worked First Watch before, so that was not the issue. My daughter was an adult and out of the house by then, so that wasn't the issue either. The issue was, I thought it was a bad idea to assign the newest, most inexperienced Lieutenant the responsibility of the entire Institution overnight, but I get it. In their minds, I dared to skip a step; to skip the line. They wanted me to suffer. They wanted me to fail and to regret my decision. Sadly, that was just the start of it.

I left Central Operations and went directly to see the Chief Deputy Warden to ask why I was assigned to First Watch.

"Because they're haters, they're mad, and they want to see you fail!" I could always count on girlfriend to keep it real. Several of them reviewed the hiring package to see if I hooked you up. They were mad when they found out you were number one in the interview, she laughed. Look, I can make a phone call if you would like. Make them give you a job change, but it's not going to help you earn their respect! Listen, we're from the Dino. We're from the street. Nobody has ever given us anything. You know how to handle yourself. Beat them at their own game."

I felt much better when I left her office. Her words played over and over in my head. "Beat them at their own game."

Yea, that's what I'll do. I thought to myself. I'll beat them at their own game!

I am sure I was assigned to First Watch as punishment by those who wanted me to fail. Fortunately, for me, and to their dismay, it had the opposite effect. I loved being the First Watch, Watch Commander, and I flourished. It allowed me to hone my supervisory skills without any pressure from the administrative staff. It taught me how to make quick, decisive, concise decisions without anyone's opinion or input. I didn't have any incidents or Rules Violation Reports to distract me. Although I could call the Administrative Officer of the Day, Custody Captain, or the Associate Warden for advice, it was generally frowned upon. Unless someone was dead, or dying, escaped or the joint was literally on fire, you better not wake them up in the middle of the night. So, making tough decisions became second nature. It also gave me time to read the Title 15, which is CDCR's bible. When I was new in the Department, I worked First Watch as an Officer. Now, I was the First Watch, Watch Commander, in charge and responsible for the entire Institution. I had come full circle.

For as long as I could remember, morale was always an issue in the Institution. On First Watch, it was worse. Usually, the Warden set the tone for the Institution, but on First Watch that was the Watch Commander's responsibility. Through the years, I worked for good and bad Wardens. Some were so bad, that the sick leave call-ins would skyrocket. No one wanted to work for a bad Warden. Some made you want to work harder because you felt like you were part of a team, part of a family. I wanted to be the type of Supervisor everyone wanted to work for. I wanted to be the type of Supervisor who made them feel like they were part of the correctional family. Supervision became my superpower. I loved it. As a Supervisor, I could be a leader and inspire staff. I had the opportunity to teach and felt it was my duty to do so. I believe you do not necessarily get what you want, but you always get what you work for. I was willing to work my ass off for it. I set out to raise the morale on First Watch.

I started a walking program. I let staff bring their tennis shoes to work. Every night we would lace up and walk four laps around the Institution. The walking program served several purposes, and it supported good health. It helped fight the weight gain that usually came with working First Watch. It kept staff from sleeping on duty and kept them alert. It fostered camaraderie, as staff had to relieve their peers from their assigned posts to participate.

We had ice cream socials. Some nights I would provide food: sub sandwiches, chips, fruit, and drinks. We had a barbecue competition, and the winner won bragging rights. I congratulated staff for everything, both institutional and outside achievements as well. I announced the birth of babies and college graduation over the institutional radio. I gave out attaboys like skittles and pats on the back as frequently as I could. I wrote letters of appreciation or accomplishment for those who didn't call in sick or went above or beyond their duties, to be put in their personnel files. I decided I would rather ask for forgiveness than permission. Nobody was there to tell me what I could not do, so I did absolutely everything! The staff loved it and so did I. William one, over and out became my catchphrase. Above all, I always called in advance of an inspection. It was never my desire to catch anyone sleeping. Who would that benefit? Certainly not I. Certainly not the Institution.

I was assigned to First Watch for nine months insulated and protected. I was sad when it was time to go. My First Watch rotation was over and I received a job change to Second Watch. I was going back to Charlie yard, back to Jurassic Park.

After being a Lieutenant for almost a year, my confidence was at an all-time high. The opportunity I had on First Watch to make decisions and lead my subordinates had given me the confidence I needed. I was a little apprehensive about my new position. Working Second Watch on such a volatile yard would require something I was not sure I had yet developed while insulated on First Watch, but I knew I would give it my best try. I figured, if I encountered any problems, at least I would have the full weight of my peers as well as the administration to assist me.

The one thing about LAC is when anybody was in trouble or needed help, the cavalry would come running. After all, we were a family . . . or at least that's what I thought.

Monday morning, I reported to my new assignment on Charlie yard. The day started just like a normal prison day. I arrived during chow release. The inmates were being released from their respective buildings, walking counterclockwise on the roadway to the chow hall. I stood on the yard for a few minutes taking it all in. Also allowing the inmates as well as staff the opportunity to see the new Lieutenant. I assumed my position, read and signed my post orders, and started my day.

The day was mostly uneventful, as we crawled toward the end of the shift. Then the alarm in housing unit one was activated and simultaneously the yard alarm was activated too.

What I learned after years of watching Lieutenants work, is it was best for the Lieutenant not to respond to the alarm. First, allow the Sergeant and staff to quell the disturbance. Then, when the incident has died down, if you'd like to see what transpired, you can respond. Although it is usually not necessary, as there are two Sergeants assigned to each yard. Also, I witnessed multiple Lieutenants as well as administrative staff, respond to the facility depending on the severity of the incident, after the announcement is made on the institutional radio identifying the disturbance. With that in mind, I stepped outside the office to observe the incident from afar and to wait for the cavalry to arrive. But the cavalry never came.

Not only did no additional Lieutenants respond, but not even the Lieutenant from Delta yard, which was Charlie yard's sister facility, respond. Nobody came. No response. No help. But wasn't that the code? I witnessed it a million times over the years. Didn't they want to help me? Didn't they want me to succeed? Well, I guess I had gotten my answer and I was devastated.

I was heartbroken, disappointed but more than that, I was angry. After I wrapped up the incident, I gathered myself and all the righteous indignation I could muster and marched down to Daniel's office. If nobody else came, he should have come. He should have been the Lone Ranger.

By the time I arrived at his office, I was enraged. I finally stood in front of Daniel as he sat behind his desk. What was that look on his face? Was that a kind of "I told you so" expression on his face? I opened my mouth to curse him out, but my voice cracked. I was so hurt; all I could do was cry. My false bravado crumbled so fast it scared me. The only thing I managed to choke out between sobs was, "Why didn't you come to help me?"

He began stuttering as he rose to his feet, "Baby, baby, baby, he stuttered. I'm sorry, there's no excuse. I should have come; we should have come. I'm so sorry. It won't happen again."

When he was finished talking, I said, "I thought we were better than that!"

"We are, I swear, we are."

Okay, we'll see, I thought to myself. I straightened my shoulders and went back to work.

When my next incident occurred, once again I stood in front of the office and watched the gate. I needed to see if what he said was true. All the Lieutenants ran through, first one after the other, including Daniel. It felt like the cavalry running to my rescue.

CHAPTER 15

THE BREAKFAST CLUB

The Breakfast Club consisted of the top Lieutenants at the Institution, most of whom were Black. Although that was not a rule of membership, only a few other Lieutenants were ever truly welcomed at the table. As a result, they had the highest seniority. They had a combined total of over one hundred years of experience working in California prisons. They came from Institutions all over the state to work at LAC when it was activated. There was nothing they did not know, and nothing they could not do. It was their jockeying position, their place on the totem pole. If prison was a university, they were the big men on campus. They enjoyed everything that entailed, and seniority meant everything to them.

Pragmatically, seniority determined their annual salary. As a Lieutenant with a high seniority number, depending on how much overtime they worked they could more than double their annual salary. Most of them earned more than the Warden. Although they met the criteria to promote to Captain, they didn't, because of the prestige, as well as the money. Once you are promoted to management level, a Captain or above, you no longer could work overtime and become a salaried employee.

As a manager, no matter how many hours you worked your salary stayed the same.

They thought of themselves as elite; the top dogs. Every weekend the Breakfast Club would stop at the cafeteria to chop it up. It was not unusual for some of them to stay there all day. There was no administrative staff on the weekend, so who was going to tell them they couldn't? There were a few managers that made several futile attempts, but they tried and failed. There wasn't a reason they couldn't. Lieutenants are mobile units. They could come and go on their facilities as they pleased. There are two Sergeants assigned to each facility that ran the daily activities on each yard. The Lieutenants usually stayed in their office doing paperwork and conducting Rules Violation Report hearings. If the Lieutenant was truly needed, he could easily be reached by radio or telephone. However, the Facility Sergeants were well-trained not to call the Lieutenant via institutional radio or there would be hell to pay. If the situation warranted the presence of the Lieutenant, it would take five minutes from the cafeteria, via golf cart to reach any facility.

The most senior Lieutenants left the facilities and yards when they had enough seniority to do so. They went to special assignments like Institutional Service Training, Inmate Assignments, and Central Operations. I didn't blame them. After decades on those hot, gritty yards who could? Some of the OG Lieutenants stayed, unable to give up the fight. They clearly suffered for it. They were the grumpiest and most disillusioned. Just like that old guard at DVI all those years ago. It was a catch-22. Stay or go. Each made his choice. When my turn came what would I choose? I already knew. I would get off those yards as quickly as possible.

When I came along, there had not been a female member of the Breakfast Club for quite a while, and when there was, she was a token. They had no intention of allowing me to become a member of their elite boys' club. However, after the stunt they pulled by not responding to my incident and the conversation between me and Daniel, they probably didn't have a choice. I am sure that's the only reason, I became a member of the Breakfast Club. Yes, I was most likely a token, but at that time, I didn't care.

Truth be told, it did not take long for me to grow tired of their shenanigans. Their constant griping and complaining about every new program or procedure. Their attempts to elevate themselves and their status above everybody else, especially managers. To them, managers were the enemy. Who they were, and what they did, was something else entirely. Most of them lacked personal and professional integrity. They were part of the good old boys' club on steroids. I lost respect for them rather quickly. I am sure they never noticed. I understood why they didn't want me around. Their misogyny was thick and rampant. They were predatory. The enthusiastic, young, new female recruits did not stand a chance; like a deer in headlights, merely, their playthings. Nobody was off-limits. Not even the wives of their subordinates.

Unfortunately, due to their inexperience or desire for an easier assignment they would easily fall into their trap. A few job changes benefiting them, and they would buy right into it and begin playing the game. "Oh, I'm so and so's girl, (insert Supervisor's name here)." You would see them perched high on the back of a Supervisor's golf cart. Their legs crossed with a smug look on their face as if to say, "Don't hate the player, hate the game!" It made them difficult to supervise, and even harder to discipline. When they were in trouble, their advocate would call me and ask me to go easy on them. If a Supervisor gave them a low annual personnel score, they would ask me to change it. They weren't doing them any favors but were willing to do almost anything to manipulate them so they could control them. Everyone knew who was and who wasn't playing the game. Those girls rarely promoted. There was no benefit to promoting in their minds. Too much work, not enough glory. You would see new recruits playing that same old game year after year. Decade after decade.

The girls that came before them had typically married someone by then, usually, another Officer, if they were lucky. If not, they were relegated to being someone's long-term mistress with their reputation in tatters or someone's baby mama or someone's "work wife," while the real wife sat at home in a big house, driving a Lexus or Benz, none the wiser.

There were incidents of girls engaging in screaming matches or coming to fisticuffs in the parking lot or on the job site fighting over some Lieutenant. Several women had children with multiple Supervisors and two or more women had children with the same man. To say it made for interesting situations and inappropriate incidents is an understatement. It often felt like living in a telenovela or a real-life soap opera. As the World Turns: Prison Edition. It was sad really. I pitied them. So, I tried not to hate the player, but I absolutely hated the game.

I realized early on that game was not for me. I intended to work hard and promote, as quickly, and as often as possible. What had I expected? Not that level of shenanigans and tomfoolery.

Despite the Breakfast Club, a shift took place in me, either between promoting to a Correctional Counselor or Correctional Lieutenant. I was proud of my chosen profession. I enjoyed my job, as well as most of my correctional family. We were dysfunctional, like most families, but when the chips were down, ultimately, they would have your back.

When I traveled during my career, as soon as people found out I worked in a prison, no matter what anybody else did for a living, the conversation would focus on me and my career. People were naturally curious.

"You work in a women's prison, right?" they asked.

"No, I work in a Level IV men's prison."

"Aren't you scared?"

"Everyday."

It could go on like that all night. Questions about things they saw on Oz, Law & Order, movies, and various cop shows. I would play along, answer their questions until I got bored, and then put a stop to it. Inevitably, over time I did not want to talk about it as much. I got tired of talking about work when I just wanted to vacation and relax like everybody else. It started to feel like what I did for a living was all I was. Nobody really wanted to get to know me. They were just interested in the salacious, sensationalism of what I did for a living. When I could not stand one more story about prison life, I stopped telling people what I did for a living. I made up different careers depending on the circle I was in. I would usually default to; I'm a counselor, a teacher, or I work for the state. All of which was true, in a way.

Working in prison changes your life. It damages you. Anyone who says it does not is not telling the truth. It changes the way you see the world, and not for the better. You see the worst in people, daily. So it teaches you to always look for the worst in people. You become hyper-vigilant, with your back against the wall, and facing the door. You are always waiting for the next shoe to drop or watching out for people trying to take advantage of you. It diminishes your trust and makes it difficult to accept people at face value or give them the benefit of the doubt. You are always staying "correctionally aware," and trying never to be a sitting duck.

It is exhausting, and it makes it difficult to make new friends. So, your world shrinks. It gets smaller. Besides my family, all my friends also worked in prison. They understood how hard it was to relate to people. Always being on guard and on yellow alert can take its toll physically, and mentally.

SENIOR HEARING OFFICER (SHO)

I loved being a Correctional Lieutenant. The absolute best part of the job was being a Senior Hearing Officer. Every inmate has due process rights when they receive a Rules Violation Report, and throughout the disciplinary process. A Senior Hearing Officer must ensure an inmate's due process rights are met.

In fact, in a prison, a Senior Hearing Officer is the judge and jury. Lieutenants are required to attend the Correctional Lieutenant's Academy in Stockton, California, to learn how to effectively and efficiently perform their duties. The California Code of Regulations, Title 15 is their Departmental bible. It is updated, printed, and redistributed annually because prison policies and procedures are constantly evolving and changing. To be an effective Senior Hearing Officer you must know it like the back of your hand and constantly use it as a reference guide. Each Lieutenant is required to adjudicate three Rules Violation Reports per shift and in the allotted time frame, as inmates have a right to a speedy and expeditious hearing. If an RVR is not adjudicated in time, the inmate cannot be held accountable for the infraction. To lose a Rules Violation Report due to not hearing it in a timely manner, is a cardinal sin. I enjoyed being a Senior Hearing Officer so much, that not only would I do the required three per shift, but I would also adjudicate whatever else was in danger of being lost due to time constraints. Sometimes, all my overtime would purely consist of me conducting hearings.

I studied the Title 15 for hours. If it was not in the Title 15, I did not do it. I was a subject matter expert and could quote it to the letter. I always ensured that my judgments were appeal-proof. Oh, they would try me, but they were rarely successful. There were times when a new Captain disagreed with my judgment and assessments and attempted to overturn my ruling. I wouldn't have it! I would go over their heads to the disciplinary Department in Sacramento and be proven right each time. Sometimes, during a hearing, I would have a sneaking suspicion that one inmate was attempting to take the rap for his cellmate, who probably had a pending release date. The new Rules Violation Report judgment would add additional time to his sentence. If I could not prove it without a shadow of a doubt, depending on the infraction or Rules Violation Report and the inmate's disciplinary history, I might allow it or I might not. If it was a low-level, nonviolent infraction and someone was held accountable justice was served.

As I began promoting up the chain of command at LAC, other women did the same. Until finally, I was no longer the only Black female Lieutenant. My good friend Stacey was promoted to Lieutenant as well. We became a force to be reckoned with. Stacey and I were both from the Inland Empire. We had attended the same high school. We had not seen each other in years but reconnected when we both found ourselves at LAC.

What are the odds of meeting an old high school friend, in prison? It turned out to be very common. Since California State Prison – Los Angeles County was Los Angeles County's only state prison—most staff were from Los Angeles, the Inland Empire, or surrounding areas. Many had transferred there from Institutions all over California. The camaraderie was unlike anything I had ever experienced, before or since. Sometimes, it felt like one big family reunion. It made sense, if you worked in prison and wanted to stay close to home and to your family and friends, you would want to work at LAC.

Stacey and I were promoted through the ranks together. By the time I was a Lieutenant for a year, so was she. Stacey enjoyed being a Senior Hearing Officer as much, if not more, than I did. So, sometimes we would tag-team a facility. When we arrived on the yard to conduct hearings, it wasn't unusual to hear an inmate yell, "Uh oh here comes trouble!" But most of the time, they'd yell, "Here comes, Judge Judy and Judge Maybelline!" We enjoyed it. It made us laugh, and sometimes it was impossible to find something to make you laugh in prison. We were fair, firm, and we had fun. If you walked onto the yard during one of our hearing sessions, you may see the inmates sitting on the bench in front of the office awaiting their turn. They looked like birds on a wire. They knew we were fair, most often they would give up, plead guilty and throw themselves at the mercy of the court before the hearing would even start. Even then, we would give them their time, to ensure their due process was never violated. We were consistent in our judgments, always maintaining our professionalism and ensuring that our final judgments were appeal-proof. We developed such a reputation that inmates would often beg us to adjudicate their hearings. After completing our hearings on one yard, we would be off the next.

There is an expression in prison, "Lieutenant is the best-kept secret in the State!" Anybody lucky enough to be a Lieutenant knew it was the absolute truth.

The people I befriended while I worked in prison taught me many valuable lessons; but mostly, they kept me human. They kept me on my toes and plenty of times they kept me safe.

I met Debra during one of those times. She transferred to LAC a few years earlier. She was a spitfire. A little woman with a big personality and a bigger mouth. Her reputation preceded her. I did not like her even before I met her. She transferred directly into a position on the Security Squad and that was never done. The rumor was it was not what she knew, but who she knew. I didn't like that one bit. By the time I was a Lieutenant, she was a Sergeant. Our paths crossed one night on Third Watch. I was the Watch Commander, and she was the hospital Sergeant. When the alarm was activated indicating a disturbance, I responded. An inmate was refusing his evening medications. Usually, when that happened, the inmate would be subdued and placed in five-point restraints, so the nurse could administer his medication. It was an exhausting and lengthy process, and Officers were always in danger of being hurt. Sergeant Debra talked to, cajoled, and commanded that inmate to submit to handcuffs and acquiesce to his medications. It took her forty-five minutes, but she got the job done. Had that been a male Officer, I know for sure it would have been the hard way, because for most male Officers that was the only way they knew. Women proved time and time again, to be better communicators and better at getting inmates to do what they were told. Regarding Deb, I should have never judged a book by its cover.

After that incident, Deb and I became fast friends. It turned out that we had much more in common than not. She worked harder for me than anyone else. She was always an asset to my team.

If a prison could have a prom queen, Debra was ours. It was not unusual to hear her loudmouth refrain, "Hey boo!" to both inmates and staff alike. So much so that the inmates started calling her, Sergeant Boo. I hated either walking onto or exiting a yard with her. The inmates would see, or better yet hear her coming and would rush to the gate just to be in her presence. She would often stop to talk to them. As I usually kept walking. I never understood how she remembered most of their names, but she did. By the time she was done holding court, I would already be through the gate holding it open for her and trying to hurry her up. "Bye boo!" she would yell to no one in particular. And in unison, the inmates would respond, "Bye Boo!" and we would finally continue on our way. It was a spectacle. I loathed any inmate's attention and would go to great lengths to avoid it. I hated it. There was always a spotlight shining on her. I never tried to dim her light. I just wanted to avoid the glare.

Deb and I would hang out after work. We made it a tradition to have drinks and dinner together every Tuesday night. We would meet at a restaurant to have cocktails and commiserate about the topic of the day, mostly working in prison. She was a great friend and knowing her made life in prison, so much more bearable.

Technically, I was a Lieutenant for three years. Although during the last year, I was an acting Captain. So, it made sense for me to take the state promotional examination for Captain. I was successful. Once again, I had to decide on my career. I had to decide if I wanted to give up overtime again as well as my position in the Institution. By that time, I had been a Lieutenant just long enough to have earned some respect and to have gained some seniority. If I were promoted to Captain, I would start over again. At the bottom. I would have a mountain of additional responsibilities, including more staff to manage. This time the decision was not that difficult. I was getting close to the end of my career. So, I was looking at the long-term benefits.

In the short term, I wouldn't be able to work overtime anymore. As a result, my annual salary would decrease quite a bit. In the long term, however, my pension would be based on a Captain's salary. I would earn more overall for the rest of my life. It was a no-brainer. I promoted. I became the only Black female Captain at LAC. Once again, standing on the shoulders of all the women who blazed the trail for me.

CHAPTER 16

CAPTAIN

There are two types of Captains in an Institution: Correctional Captain and Facility Captain. At LAC, there are two Correctional Captains: a Healthcare Captain, and a Custody Captain; as well as four Facility Captains, for a total of six positions.

Captains run the facilities as well as the Institution. They are in the first position on the management ladder. As a result, they ensure the Institution runs smoothly and the staff do their jobs. As I tested for both, I could be assigned to either position. However, I was assigned to the Custody Captain position. The Custody Captain has the most responsibility of any Captain in the Institution. He is responsible for everything, except for the facilities, or healthcare.

I was assigned to manage Central Operations—it consists of: visiting, sally ports, all areas of ingress and egress, towers, electrified fence, all institutional counts, and all areas outside the secured perimeter fence i.e., warehouse, carport, etc. Additionally, all staff hiring, and transfers, as well as ensuring the Institution is always appropriately staffed, along with the Minimum Support Facility (MSF), which houses two hundred low-level offenders was my responsibility. I knew it would be the biggest challenge of my career. I always wanted to be at the table where decisions were made. This was my chance.

Custody Captain pushed me to the top of the food chain among my peers. I made most of the decisions regarding the everyday running of the Institution. I would also take the blame when things went wrong.

Like many high-achieving African Americans, as well as women in positions of authority, I suffered from imposter syndrome. Imposter syndrome is a psychological pattern in which an individual doubts their skills, talents, or accomplishments and has a persistent internalized fear of being exposed as a fraud. Despite external evidence of their competence, those experiencing this phenomenon remain convinced that they are frauds and do not deserve all they have achieved. I was always on pins and needles, just waiting for the next shoe to drop. Although it never really did. I believed in myself and what I had to offer from the very beginning of my career. I knew I would promote up the chain. I was intelligent. I had an impeccable work ethic and was proud of my professional integrity. I always did the right thing, because it was simply the right thing to do.

I was very controlling; always trying to control my environment. Those should have been positive attributes in such a harsh environment, but I was a woman, so would "they" see it? Would they support me? If my past experiences were any indication, I already knew my answer.

Once I was promoted to Captain, everything started all over again. The stares, the whispers, the judgment. The "Who does she think she is?" There were some who no longer associated with me. Some no longer spoke to me. Usually, it was the people I had to supervise and manage. Did common decency and home training stop at a particular classification? It sure felt like it. It was the same shit, different day, and from the same people. Maybe, but this time was different. I did not stumble. I did not miss a step, because this time I did not care. Of course, my membership in the Breakfast Club was unilaterally revoked! I had moved another rung up the ladder past them. I was ahead of them in the chain of command. I was their Supervisor and was required to manage them. I was back at square one. As far as staff goes everything seemed much worse. It didn't help matters that I started as an acting Captain before I was promoted in earnest. They were brutal. I was isolated and found myself lonely on many occasions. I couldn't quite hang out with management yet, as I didn't know them. My subordinates didn't necessarily want to hang out with me either, no matter how many years we had known each other. I felt the same. I was the same. Why were they treating me differently? There weren't many people to talk to at work. No one to go to lunch with. I missed the camaraderie of being a Counselor. It made a big difference in my love of the job. There weren't many things to love about this job, and that was one of them. So, I fell into my usual routine. I put my head down and retreated into my work . . . something I knew . . . something I understood . . . something I was good at. I came in early and was the last manager to leave at night. I easily worked twelve-hour days and often came in on my days off.

Thank God for my girlfriends! My tribe! They were a group of intelligent, fiercely loyal Black women who had moved up the chain of command before me, beside me, and behind me. They saved me. We became a unit. They became my support system. A sisterhood. It was four of us: one Chief Deputy Warden, two Captains, and one Sergeant. We were a force of nature. On any given day you would see us trooping down those long hot roadways or driving our golf cart en route to handle institutional business. The CDW was my friend and mentor. We had met in 9th grade but hadn't seen each other again until we both showed up at LAC. It was the same for the Captain. We had gone to high school together and ended up in the same career, at the same Institution. The Sergeant was the baby of our tribe. In her past life, she was a nurse. When she found out how much Correctional Officers are paid, she switched careers midstream. She loves to tell the story of how we met. She walked onto Charlie yard one day and encountered me sitting on the bench in front of the program office, in my business suit, with my dolly and boxes teaming with central files. As I thought of myself as the self-appointed institutional greeter, I said, "Welcome to CSP-LAC, my name is Counselor Cromwell. If you need anything, please let me know!" Her response was, "I certainly will, because I want to be just like you when I grow up."

They were intimidated by us. They called us everything but a child of God. They said everything we did was reverse racism. They called us sexist, and dykes or lesbians. As if the latter was an insult. It was not. They said we promoted because we hated men, or worse, because we wanted to be one. Of course, they didn't say it to our faces, but they said it, nonetheless.

Many of the Black male Supervisors that I encountered were sexist. While many of the White Supervisors were also sexist, with a little racism thrown in for good measure. Not all, but more than enough. Of course, as a Black woman, I was more disappointed in the Black Supervisors and managers. They should have mentored us, encouraged us, and defended us, but instead, they tried to stop us, demean us, and limit our progress.

There was one Sergeant who was extremely jealous and hateful. He was never very successful in his career. He was a closeted alcoholic. However, since everyone was aware he was an alcoholic, he was not that closeted. Interestingly enough, we were friends in a past life. Our families occasionally went to dinner together, hung out, and just enjoyed each other's company. Unfortunately, after his wife died, he changed. He became bitter and unpleasant. I guess we became the embodiment of all he'd lost and his professional failures. He nicknamed us the "Black Bitch Man Hater's Club!" It was the height of racism, sexism, and misogyny. Of course, he was never brave enough to say it to our faces, most cowards aren't, but we heard the snickers behind our backs. Occasionally, someone would tell us as if they were telling us some conspiratorial secret. We heard. We knew.

Interestingly, it did not defeat us. Which, of course, is what it was meant to do. To knock us down a peg or two. Instead, it became our badge of honor. Honestly, we thought it was hilarious that those men, who thought so highly of themselves were so obviously jealous of a bunch of women. It spurred us on. It made us do more, reach higher, promote more often and faster. It made us stronger than we may have otherwise been. We mentored those women who wanted to come along. What is that phrase, "Each one teach one?" And we did. We became the face of the Institution. Everywhere we went they knew our names.

Since my first assignment as acting Captain was Custody Captain, I was responsible for the Institution. The senior Captains were not interested in the job. It required long hours, as the Custody Captain was often the first to arrive and the last to leave. Each morning during the daily staff briefing the Custody Captain was required to report on the operation of the Institution including the previous evening/night inmate counts, the hiring of Correctional Officers for Second Watch, and the appropriate staffing of the Institution. It was a lot.

At the Custody Captain level, one of my chief duties was managing programs and as the Chief Disciplinary Officer of the Institution. I was charged with the evaluation, and necessary discipline of wayward staff. The programs were the easy part. Disciplining staff, not so much. There is a long, labor-intensive disciplinary process utilized by the Department of Corrections and Rehabilitation. At each step in the disciplinary process, staff has appeal rights and labor union representation. I understood it, but I didn't like it. The fact is that the State of California pays thousands of dollars to recruit, educate and train correctional staff, so it is their desperate desire to retain as much of their investment as possible. There were limited, almost extreme circumstances that allowed for the firing of a Peace

Officer. It made it almost impossible to change their attitudes, to teach them professional responsibilities and personal integrity. If they had not joined the Department with a firmly established work ethic, there wasn't much I could teach them. What I was quite often left with was ineffectual people in a position of authority over others, in a profession they had no business in, and it was my job to manage them. That was the part of the job I hated the most, managing staff.

Early in my assignment as Custody Captain, I encountered a problem. My peers, the other Captains, would often refer their staff to me because they did not, or were afraid to discipline them. Especially female staff, who were usually out of compliance with the grooming standard policy. Many of them would attempt to skirt the dress code because they put more value in looking good than professionalism and safety. They would come into the Institution with ponytails swinging, colored nail polish, and dangling earrings and jewelry. All of which was against the dress code and could be dangerous. My peers went through great pangs to not appear to be "the bad guy" as they would tell me when I called them out on their bullshit. We were paid handsomely to do our job. If enforcing the policies made us the bad guy, so be it. They seemed to disagree, but did not mind making me the bad guy instead. They preferred to be friends with their subordinates. Of course, that made it almost impossible for them to be impartial and discipline them when necessary.

The disciplinary code was strict, but the process was not difficult. The offending staff would receive a verbal warning and be told how to correct the problem.

Then a follow-up meeting was held to ensure they complied. If the staff was still non-compliant, then a written warning was given. By then, most staff would acquiesce and comply. However, there was always a percentage of staff who would dig in their heels and choose that particular hill to die on. When that was the case, I would elevate the disciplinary process to the next level. It was laborious and taxing. I was willing to do it and became quite good at it. I became known for staff discipline.

I had very little sympathy for senior Officers who continually committed infraction after infraction, and who knew what they were doing was against policy yet continued to do it anyway. However, the newer, younger, unsophisticated Officers were the ones I continually trained. Even if sometimes it came back to bite me. I thought they needed to be taught and mentored into making good choices and doing the right thing. I wanted to inspire them. Unfortunately, some came into the Department with an obvious agenda, ready and willing to join the brotherhood, whatever they thought that meant. It was a real-life version of the Stanford Experiment, which was an experiment conducted in the early 70s that suggested people will readily conform to the social roles they are expected to play. Especially if the roles are as strongly stereotyped as those of Correctional Officers. They usually had an "us versus them" mentality, which made it easy for them to cross the line. Sometimes, they were my worst nightmare. They didn't seem to have a moral compass or personal integrity.

There was little I could do to change that. They would constantly, almost from the very start of their career, abuse sick leave, FMLA, leave early without being appropriately relieved of their duties, or be a no call, no show for work. When they did come to work, they did the bare minimum. They often didn't understand the consequences of their actions. Or worse, they simply didn't care. They were usually the ones I referred for administrative review. They could not be saved, and the Department should not have been the place for them.

It almost took an act of God to fire a Peace Officer. Regardless of how egregious the offense. The Department's position is that it is very expensive to recruit and train staff, so they did everything in their power to retain them. Even if it meant constant and direct supervision and discipline. All it did was foster laziness and made them a nightmare to supervise and manage.

At some point, it seemed my peers, as well as CDCR, adopted a management style, I called management avoidance. We were often instructed to train everyone, to avoid singling out the actual individual who was the problem and needed direct training or disciplining. Speaking broadly to everyone instead of directly to the person who needed to be spoken to. It was disingenuous and kept us in a constant training loop without anything being taught or accomplished.

You could never be sure the message reached the person it was intended for in the first place. I did it sometimes because I was expected to, but I hated it. What I didn't understand was how they thought you could correct a problem without directly addressing the issue.

What was worse than Correctional Officers who could not be trained to do the right thing, simply because it was the right thing to do, was the abuse of authority from Supervisors. During that time, the Institution began having issues with Supervisors not following the nepotism/fraternization policy.

D.O.M. 33010.25

Nepotism/Fraternization Policy

> *"Employees involved in personal relationships may work in the same program, section, or unit as the person with whom they have a personal relationship, however, employment settings shall not exist where an employee would; (A) work for the same Supervisor as the person whom they have a personal relationship, (B) Have a direct or indirect supervisory relationship as the person with whom they have a personal relationship, (C) Work under the hiring authority with who they have a personal relationship, regardless of Departmental separation."*

The Department was often a family affair. It was common to have husbands and wives, as well as adult children and siblings working in the same Institution. Of course, that could present challenges and become problematic for many reasons, safety and security is the biggest issue. The policy clearly states employees involved in personal relationships cannot work in the same area, or for the same Supervisor and cannot supervise each other. However, some Supervisors began ignoring the policy and began hiring husband and wife teams on overtime, assigning them to the same areas, particularly the outside hospital detail. When I would inquire about it, they would say, "but they're not on the same floor of the hospital," or "they are not covering the same inmate!" They knew the policy, they simply chose to ignore it.

Two Lieutenants were the most egregious offenders. Both had wives who were Correctional Officers. One Lieutenant began redirecting his spouse to his facility. I arrived on Facility A one day, only to find the Lieutenant's wife sitting on the bench outside the program office swinging her legs as if she didn't have a care in the world. Naturally, the Facility Sergeant, who was her direct Supervisor reported the problem. That morning the Lieutenant called the Watch Office and had his wife re-directed to his facility. Even worse, the Lieutenant prohibited the Sergeant from assigning his wife any duties and intimidated him into not reporting the situation to management. As Custody Captain, all hiring and the redirection of staff was my direct responsibility. I called the office to find out why the Officer was redirected to work indirectly for her husband. The Watch Sergeant's response was, "he gave me a direct order." The Watch Sergeant felt he was in a precarious position, so he simply followed orders. Without even setting foot in the office, I turned on my heels and marched back to my office. After giving the Watch Sergeant training, I wrote a memorandum. The memo directly named the Lieutenant and his spouse. Of course, that is not how it is usually done. Following the

Institution's unwritten guidelines, I was expected to "train" all Supervisors on the nepotism/fraternization policy. I did not even consider such a farce. How dare he abuse his authority and intimidate not one, but two Sergeants to redirect his wife to his yard? Not on my watch! I gave the completed memo to the Watch Commander, who was shaking his head and nervously laughing, as he read it. I demanded it to be posted in the Watch Sergeant's office, so it would never happen again. Once it was posted, I dared anyone to remove it. As soon as the Watch Sergeant contacted the Officer via institutional radio and redirected her to another post, the word was out.

The Associate Warden of Central Operations, my direct Supervisor, immediately called me for a meeting. During the meeting, he asked me to remove the memo and provide documented training to all supervisory staff. I respectfully refused. He understood my position and never gave me a direct order to do so. The Lieutenant filed a complaint against me accusing me of singling him out for workplace harassment. Of course, he lost his complaint. My memo remained posted in the Watch Office. There were no more issues with Supervisors redirecting their spouses again, or husbands and wives being assigned to the same hospital detail. At least not while I was Custody Captain.

OPERATION DISCONNECT

In the Department, contraband is a big problem. Drugs, cell phones, and other contraband is rampant and coming into the prison at an alarming rate. Gangs control drugs and weapons. Illicit drugs negatively impacted all aspects of prison life. Drugs were the reasons for fights, assaults, riots, and murders. It was difficult to control an inmate under the influence. It was nearly impossible to stem the tide of drugs being introduced into the prison. There were so many ways they got in. They usually came in through receiving and release in inmates' property, through the mail, or through visiting. On the minimum facility, which is the closest yard to the street, it wasn't unusual for them to be simply tossed over the fence or lobbed onto the yard inside tennis balls. Unfortunately, a big source of the introduction of drugs and contraband into the Institution was due to staff bringing it in. Staff would bring prohibited items into the Institution to inmates for several reasons: 1) the offending staff was having a sordid, illicit relationship with the inmate, or: 2) they were being paid to bring in the contraband. It happened so frequently that sometimes it seemed like an everyday occurrence.

To combat this, the Department developed a new policy and procedure code named: Operation Disconnect.

As the Custody Captain in charge of Central Operations, it was my direct responsibility to develop the institutional strategy to achieve the goal of stemming the tide of drugs and cell phones being introduced into the Institution by staff. I saw staff bring in everything including, money, food, cigarettes, cell phones, and drugs. Once, a nurse brought food into the Correctional Treatment Center to have a picnic with her inmate lover. They were caught picnicking on a dirty blanket in the linen closet of the center. Staff have lost their jobs, their livelihoods, their families, and even their freedom.

Once a month we would conduct systematic, surprise inspections of all staff entering the Institution. Each month the inspection would be conducted in a different area. The locations of the operations were: the administrative lobby, to get all non-custody staff who worked in the administration building; the entrance building and sally port, to get all staff entering the secure perimeter; Central Control, to get all staff who worked on Facilities A and B, including Central Operations; and finally Complex Control, to get all staff who worked on Facilities C and D. Operation Disconnect was conducted on a rotational basis.

Once staff became aware of the operation, we had to change our tactics. As they would attempt to evade the process. Some of them would hang around in the parking lot. They would try to leave the Institution and call in sick from their cars. Sometimes they would stay in the administration building and call in late to their assigned position. We would have to stop them at the front gate. Sometimes we would send an Officer to check the parking lot and administration building.

Operation Disconnect was a long, tedious process, as most things are in CDCR. It took a month to coordinate and a half-day to execute. We recovered cigarettes, cell phones, illicit photographs, excessive money, and drugs. Drugs were the most difficult to recover from staff, as they could be secreted in private areas of their bodies that we could not search. However, if a female was suspected of having possession of illegal contraband and agreed to submit to a full-body search, a female member of Operation Disconnect would conduct a strip search in a facility bathroom. That did not happen often. Although I was a manager, I was always embarrassed for the individual. I attempted to leave them with as much dignity as possible, but I never understood why? Why did they do it in the first place? Why jeopardize your entire life for an inmate? Every incident would inevitably take me back to my friend Reva, sitting on the floor of her apartment crying. Why they did it was a rhetorical question, because there was no logical answer.

I was Custody Captain for over a year. After Lieutenant, it was my favorite position. The Custody Captain knew everything, and was involved in everything. Very little happened in the Institution without my knowledge or my input.

As I walked across Facility A one day, en route back to my office, I heard an inmate on the other side of the fence say.

"Hey Captain Cromwell, long time, no see."

I didn't stop walking as I didn't make a habit of talking to inmates unless I needed to.

But he was persistent, "Congratulations on your promotion."

Now, that made me stop. Did I recognize that voice? As I began looking through the fence at a sea of inmates' faces, I knew it was him before our eyes met. Washer! I stared at him a moment. He looked the same, except for his salt-and-pepper hair and his graying beard. Had it been that long? At least ten years. I walked over to him.

"You look old," I said.

"Yea, it's the gray hair," he chuckled.

"How long have you been back?"

"A couple of weeks. Tim and Kalen knew I was here. They didn't tell you?"

"No." They hadn't told me.

"Good to see you."

I continued on my way. Wow! I didn't know what to think or what to say. I thought I would never see him again, but there he was.

As I entered Central Operations, I stopped at Inmate Assignments. Kalen was the Lieutenant assigned to that area. He was a member of the Breakfast Club, but I didn't hold it against him.

"Hey, Kalen, I see homeboy is on Facility A," I said. He knew just who I was referring to.

"Oh, you finally ran into him?" He chuckled. "Tim and I ran into him a few weeks ago."

"Why didn't you tell me?"

"I wanted you to see him for yourself."

I could respect that.

"Have him escorted to my office." Ten minutes later, Inmate Washer was sitting across from me on the other side of my desk. We made small talk for a couple of minutes. He told me both his mother and father had died while he was in Pelican Bay. I told him my daughter was grown and had finally left home. Then I got to the point.

"Why?" I still wanted to know what happened all those years ago. He hung his head.

"Yea, I fucked up. I started getting high on my own supply. Became addicted and got caught up. They kept asking me about you. So, I thought I could get a better deal. But I didn't. It didn't work and they sent me to the Bay, anyway. You didn't deserve what I did. If I could take it back, I would."

That was it. That was all there was to it.

"You're right, I didn't deserve it." I agreed. After Inmate Washer was escorted back to his yard.

"Hey Kalen, if there's a vacancy in Central Operations, give homeboy a job."

"Will do!"

And he did. I don't know why I gave him a job. I didn't have to, but for some reason, I wanted to. It meant more to him than it did to me.

Inmate Washer worked for me for a few months. We would say hello in passing. Sometimes he would stop in for a quick conversation and be on his way. I didn't know if having him around reminded me of my past; of the naïve girl, I used to be. Or, if it made me proud of how far I had come. Whatever the reason, it no longer mattered.

Once my acting time as Custody Captain was over, I was hired permanently. I was assigned everywhere in the Institution that needed a Captain. Every position, in every facility. I worked for almost every Associate Warden in the Institution. Like all classifications, the Associate Warden classification had both good and bad managers. Those that inspired you to be, and do your best. As well as those who taught you what not to do, and who not to be. Some of them made you wonder how they were promoted in the first place.

There was one Associate Warden I worked for who was the latter. He seemed to pop up at LAC out of nowhere. The rumor was he applied for the position from an outside state agency and was hired "off the street" after suing the Department.

He had no prison experience and had not been promoted through the chain of command. As a result, he had no idea what the hell he was doing. There were a few outliers like him in the Department. Thank God, there were only a few. He was obnoxious with a superiority complex. You know the type. He was convinced he was better than everyone, the smartest person in the room, based purely on his education and pedigree. He knew absolutely nothing about the job or his responsibilities. He did everything in his power to prevent me from being promoted to a full-time position. And yet, he had the nerve to always smile in my face. It reminded me of that song, "Backstabbers" by The O'Jays.

If it wasn't for our cowboy Warden, who just happened to be passing through, and who promised me he would do everything in his power to ensure I received the promotion I so clearly earned before he left LAC, I'm not entirely sure how successful he would have been in blocking me.

He often behaved as if I was his assistant. He attempted to assign me some of his duties that were clearly at the Associate Warden level. He didn't know how to do his job and had no interest in learning. He was a bullshitter of the highest degree! He was all hat and no cattle. I never met a man who loved to hear his own voice so much. He made quite a splash at LAC, and not in a good way. Once he told a classroom of correctional staff that Nazis were just a misunderstood group of people with their political point of view, which should be respected. Of course, I promptly filed a complaint against him. He also wrote a memorandum, while Associate Warden of Central Operations, banning staff from displaying a picture of the first Black President because it was "too political." That fiasco went all the way to headquarters in Sacramento. Headquarters promptly sent a memo to all Institutions that staff had the right to display a picture of President Obama in their work areas, just like every other President before him. He dared to remove my name from a report I generated and replaced it with his own. I was livid!

When I called him on it and eventually reported it to the Chief Deputy Warden and Warden, he attempted to gaslight me. He tried to convince me he had every right to do so as my Supervisor. He had blatantly stolen my intellectual property and tried to convince me it belonged to him. He taught me many lessons on what NOT to do, and how NOT to manage staff. I learned to always give my subordinates credit for a job well done. And when you receive accolades, so should your staff.

CHAPTER 17

THE FACILITIES

FACILITY A

Facility A was supposed to be a relatively short stop on my ride as a Captain. I welcomed it. I was hoping just to chill out and relax for a few months until they once again put me somewhere where I was needed. I swear, anywhere I went if there was not already an issue, an issue would develop, and A yard was no different. Facility A was the Sensitive Needs Yard (SNY), having transitioned from a Level III yard to the "honor" yard a few years before.

An SNY yard is a yard that houses inmates who are segregated from the general population for their safety. Because the inmates housed on Facility A, SNY, are required to sign a form agreeing to refrain from all gang ties, activities, and violence to be housed there, the yard was relatively quiet and tame at least by prison standards. There could be weeks without an incident or other bad behavior. There are considerably fewer Rules Violation Reports and incidents on the yard. As a result of good behavior, they were often approved for additional recreational activities. There were music concerts, comedy shows as well as visits from celebrities, as

Hollywood was a quick 60 miles to the south of the Institution. Facility A was just what I needed to decompress from the grueling responsibilities of the Custody Captain. The ladies and I enjoyed A yard immensely. We would often join in the approved activities from time to time. You could find us working behind the scenes, and sometimes swaying to the music while enjoying a concert.

I was there for two weeks before there was a problem. Unfortunately, on Facility A, in Housing Units 4 and 5 is where the Administrative Segregation Unit was located. The Facility A Captain was responsible for it as well.

ADMINISTRATIVE SEGREGATION

Prisoners are placed in solitary confinement, for violent or disruptive behavior. It typically involves single-cell confinement for 23 hours daily; inmates are allowed one hour out of the cell for exercise and showers.

For the two weeks, I was assigned to the facility, inmate housing had become increasingly problematic. Especially in Administrative Segregation. More and more frequently the inmates refused to double cell. It was a departmental policy that all inmates would double cell, with few exceptions. However, many inmates found a way around that rule. Of course, the inmates preferred their own cells, who wouldn't? Many OG inmates had what's known as "Cadillac cells," where they were often housed alone. Some cells were decked out with contraband stolen over the years from their work sites as well as other inmates. Some cells were painted inside, some had checkerboard patterned floors and curtains. Staff shouldn't have allowed the contraband. And all contraband should have been confiscated during their daily cell searches. However, as with most things when staff decided to look the other way it became a bigger problem. After a while, it was easier to turn a blind eye than to have to fight to remove it.

Although the Institution was built to house 2,200 or fewer inmates, LAC was quickly approaching 5,000 inmates. Unless there was a legitimate reason for an inmate to be single-celled, i.e., assault, rape, or murder of a cellmate, they would be forced to double cell. It would be a major operation and I was responsible for its successful completion.

Once all the inmates who were refusing to double cell were identified, they were taken to classification. During classification, it was determined by the Institutional Classification Committee if there was a legitimate reason that precluded him from double celling. Usually, it was determined, as expected, that very few inmates had legitimate reasons for being single-celled. During committee, they were given a direct order to double cell. If he still refused, he was written a Rules Violation Report, if he was found guilty it would increase his sentence. It always benefited them to simply give in and take a cellmate. Most did. However, many did not. They thought of themselves as warriors and would fight us every step in the process. That was the easy part.

If by then the inmate had not taken the opportunity to surrender peacefully and accept a cellmate, we would physically force him to. At any point in the operation, the inmate could give up and agree to double cell.

I was always proud that I could get an inmate to do anything I wanted him to do. I would treat it almost like a game. Unbeknownst to the inmates, I treated them like children, and I was the parent. How could I get them to do exactly what I wanted them to do with the least amount of resistance? I would talk to them. I told them the truth. I would explain to them that if they didn't do what they were ordered to do, it would hurt them more than it would hurt me. They could either do it the hard way or the easy way, but ultimately they would do it. If we were pushed to utilize force, they would certainly live to regret it. The simple truth is what usually worked.

I always gave inmates what they had coming, if not a little bit more. I used positive reinforcement. I was fair, firm, and consistent. I earned their respect, if not their trust. I gave them their showers on time, and released them for work, yard, dayroom, and chow on time. Many, many years before, when I was the Chow Hall Officer, if they didn't steal any food, or short the chow line, I would give them the leftovers at the end of the shift. I would sarcastically brag, "I can tell an inmate to jump, and he would ask for permission to come down!" Like I said it was a game, but that worked less and less the more I promoted up the chain of command. By the time I was Captain, I was so far removed from the inmates, it no longer worked at all.

During the first day of operation single cell, the team was assembled for the grueling task of forcibly removing the inmates from their cells. The team consisted of six Officers: two shield Officers, two handcuff Officers, and two additional Officers for good measure. We lined up at the first cell. I read the inmate his rights. I requested that he voluntarily exit the cell and receive a new cell assignment and explained to him exactly what would happen if he refused. When he refused, the cell door was opened. The two shield Officers rushed into the cell, pinned the inmate down, placed him in handcuffs, and carried him out of the cell. He was placed in a holding cell for a cooling-down period. Then we moved on to the next cell. So forth and so on we went. By the time we reached the sixth cell, the inmates in the housing unit had had enough. Truth be told, so had we. They surrendered. Thank God! We were as physically spent as they were. Those were the kind of operations that usually left staff injured. It was always my desire and intent to avoid cell extractions as much as possible.

Unfortunately, no matter how much I tried to de-escalate the situation, they left us no choice. In cases like that, the inmates controlled our reactions based on their refusal to follow our direct orders. Even though they understood they had little to no choice, their ego would often get the best of them, and they would live to regret it. In the end, we prevailed. We re-housed every inmate that was designated double cell.

The Department was hard mentally, but just as hard physically. By then, my body had started to rebel and break down. I already had a case of plantar fasciitis earlier in my career, as did many of my female peers. Male work boots are not made for female feet. As a result, our arches began to deteriorate from standing for hours on concrete. I also developed bursitis in my hips, from carrying 25-40 pounds of equipment daily. Women have a lower center of gravity, so that much weight sitting directly on top of my hips was wearing them out.

Male Officers did not fare any better, as many of them had begun wearing suspenders to lift the heavy belts off their hips. They wore water packs on their backs in an attempt to stay hydrated as several passed out during the brutal heat of the summer months. They developed high cholesterol and high blood pressure.

On one occasion we found an Officer stumbling down the hallway delirious with blood pressure so high he was whisked away to the hospital via ambulance.

Everyone got fatter and fatter, as we got older and older. Of course, that just exacerbated everything; as our feet, ankles, knees, hips, and backs began to wear down and give out. Prison is a young man's game, and I wasn't young anymore. Most people think, didn't you sign up for this? Not necessarily. Human beings are not designed and built for such physical punishment, but we soldiered on, month after month, year after year, decade after decade. At this point, I was just holding on until retirement.

It was apparent that Facility A was not the place I thought it would be to rest and recuperate for even a short period. That was on me. No such place exists in a Level IV men's prison. I kept getting moved from yard to yard, assignment to assignment doing the best job I could, given the circumstances. And on each yard, the circumstances were just a little bit different.

FACILITY D

I worked on Delta yard several times throughout my career. I began as an Officer. I was assigned to Delta 2 as the Counselor and conducted hearings there. I was the facility Lieutenant, and did a very short stint as the Facility Captain. It felt like another full-circle moment, and I had plenty of those throughout my career.

Delta yard would present a unique challenge. A challenge I would need help solving. Facility D had a gang problem, as every other yard did. However, the gang problem on Delta yard was an Officer gang. There was a group of Officers who appeared to be a gang. They all wore the same hat. They wore the same flashlight on the same side of their uniform to differentiate themselves from their peers. It was the worst kept secret in the Institution. No, they were not the traditional definition of a gang. But informally, they had similarities of one, and of course, they were almost always involved in most of the use of force incidents on the yard. They behaved as if they were racking up notches on their work belts.

Week after week, the same Officers' names would be included in just about every incident, and in every report we reviewed during the weekly managerial Use of Force Committee. Somebody might make a comment or two about it, but there was never any follow-up or follow-through.

Their use of force reports would always read the same. As if they thought they discovered the ultimate way of getting away with unnecessary or excessive use of force. There was one incident on the yard, where an Officer punched an inmate so hard, that he knocked him out in the middle of the recreational yard. That of course was not taught in training. The Officer said he had simply "blacked out" during the incident and did not remember hitting the inmate. It was the talk of the Institution for weeks. He got a pat on the back from his peers for that one. It was the blatant arrogance that made me angry.

The morning I walked onto Delta yard to start my new assignment; my first stop was the Lieutenant's office. He was someone I knew and trusted.

"Good morning Kalen," I said

"Good morning," he responded.

"Okay, Kalen what do I do? How do I break up that gang?"

He smiled wryly. "Are you sure you want to do that?" He didn't pretend to not know what I was talking about.

"Yep."

"Okay, then get ready because they are going to come at you with everything they got. They're going to say you are racist (as most of them were white males). They are going to say you are sexist, that you hate men."

I heard it all before. I wasn't scared. Right was right. I couldn't live with myself if I could do something about it but didn't. He pulled out the assignment roster, and we began pouring over each assignment. It didn't take long for us to quickly identify the culprits.

"Here's what you're going to do. Job change everyone that's in an administrative position. You can't touch them if their position is based on seniority, but you can get rid of most of them!"

When we reviewed the yard assignments, they were all White Officers, except for one Black and one Hispanic Officer. Unfortunately, they were untouchable as they were in senior positions.

I was advised to pick one random Black Officer, one random Hispanic Officer and to throw in one female Officer for good measure. Job change them all at the same time. Disperse them to every yard and every shift. If anyone asked me why I chose those Officers, I would say, "for no reason." I wanted to fill my administrative positions myself, which is what they were intended for. Once they started filing their complaints and appeals, they wouldn't have a leg to stand on because I job changed every race and gender at the same time. That is exactly what I did. And when I was asked, that's exactly what I said.

He was right. They called me racist. They said it was reverse discrimination and I hated White people. They called me sexist. They said I hated men. They did not win. They lost all their complaints and appeals. It was all for show anyway. Just trying to save face. They behaved just like inmates. The union came after me. I often felt that the union was on the wrong side of right. Why try to protect Officers that gave us all a bad name? They made us all look bad. They had to tuck their tails and go to their new assignments. Not only had I won, but the Institution had won. I broke up the Officer gang on D yard. Why couldn't someone else have done it? Why was it allowed to continue, fester, and negatively impact morale?

It made me question if it was condoned. No one ever wanted the smoke. Nobody ever wanted the heat. They never wanted to be the "bad guy." I heard it repeatedly throughout my career. To that, I say this, "If you can't stand the heat, get out of the kitchen!" If you sign up to be a supervisor or a manager, then at least do the minimum requirement of the job. If you discover being a supervisor or manager is not your forté, don't promote. If you only promote for the money and prestige, you become part of the problem. I am convinced that what is needed to be a great supervisor or manager is to care about your people, and do what is right each time. Be fair. Be honest. Please do not abuse your authority. Attempting to avoid being the "bad guy" will make you an ineffectual supervisor or manager.

CHAPTER 18

HEALTH CARE

During my career, I reinvented myself many times. I thought it was the secret to longevity, to avoid burnout. It is not inconsequential that each reinvention paralleled each promotion and each job change.

I didn't enjoy being a Facility Captain. I didn't like the politics on the yards. Too many moving pieces. The constant incident packages, and Rules Violation Reports would sometimes keep me in my office well after my peers had gone home. Too many staff required disciplinary action. As the years passed, inspiring and motivating staff became increasingly difficult. As a result, more disciplinary action was necessary. However, I enjoyed being a Correctional Captain. Luckily, LAC had two positions, I had already been the Custody Captain. I would love to be the Healthcare Captain. I was still assigned to Facility D when the Healthcare Captain retired. His position was up for grabs. If I got that position, I too could be one of those Captains that sauntered into the Institution just in time for the daily briefing, and left right after the Warden in the afternoon. At least that's what I thought. Everyone would be vying for the position.

Instead of waiting for an announcement of who got the job, which is what I usually did, I met with the Associate Warden of Healthcare and directly asked for the position. As luck would have it, the AW and I were Counselors together back in the day. I asked him for a favor. Isn't that how it worked? Wasn't it based on whom you knew? Well, I knew someone and could get something I wanted. Plus, he knew me. He knew my work ethic. He knew I would work harder for him than any other Captain. It was a win-win for both of us. So why not me? Everybody was surprised when I got the job. My fellow Captains with much more seniority than I, asked for the position and were denied. It left a few of them upset and disappointed. At that point in my career, I did not care.

One of the best things about being Health Care Administration (HCA) Captain was my office was in the middle of the Institution, not on any yard. I still hated walking onto the yards. That was one less thing I had to think about. Also, the HCA Lieutenant and Sergeant usually took care of the daily execution of health and dental care in the Institution. My primary job was to attend all HCA meetings as a committee member.

The position of the HCA Captain is to: facilitate, monitor, and ensure all inmates received needed and necessary health, dental, and mental healthcare; to ensure they are present for all healthcare appointments scheduled with the Institution and community providers; to ensure proper correctional coverage of appointments; and to manage the movement and transportation of all inmates, including emergency ambulance transports. The HCA Captain is also the manager of the institutional transportation teams. As the HCA Captain is the correctional liaison between medical and custody staff, they are an integral part of all medical and dental committees and are required to attend all meetings. The HCA Captain at LAC is responsible for the Correctional Treatment Center (CTC), which is the institutional hospital, as well as each facility clinic. The HCA Captain's primary responsibility is to act as a liaison.

Through the years, CDCR was mired in lawsuits directly related to healthcare, dental and mental health. As the Department lost one lawsuit after another, healthcare and mental health were expanded. More and more laws were changed, which meant more and more policy changes in the Department. The four key lawsuits that directly impacted my job as HCA Captain were:

1. Armstrong—The Armstrong remedial plan provides specific direction regarding the disability placement program (DPP). It is the Department's set of plans, policies, and procedures to assure nondiscrimination against inmates with permanent disabilities.
2. Clark—The Clark remedial plan covers the dos and don'ts of the developmental disability program (DDP). The DDP applies to all the Department's Institutions, to all programs that the Department provides or operates, and to all inmates who have developmental disabilities.
3. Perez—This lawsuit alleges the dental care provided by CDCR is woefully inadequate. The settlement required major improvements in prisoner dental care.
4. Plata—The court placed CDCR's Healthcare delivery system into receivership. The receiver oversees all healthcare services.

Once CDCR was placed into receivership, the AW of each Institution was directly supervised by the Director of California Correctional Health Care Services in Sacramento.

To combat the backlog of unsolved cases, the State began requiring all inmates to provide a DNA sample. The law had changed many years before; however, CDCR had not yet attempted to obtain a sample from each inmate as it would be a massive undertaking. Therefore, the Department was out of compliance with the law. Of course, it became my responsibility to institute a plan of action.

At the same time, California instituted a new policy that all CDCR inmates were required to have a tuberculosis vaccination. As luck would have it the new policies began as soon as I began my new assignment as HCA Captain. Each new policy required a new operation to force every inmate into compliance. My peers were no longer salty, as they had dodged a bullet. During the DNA operation, before the start of the TB operation, the HCA Associate Warden retired. I did not begrudge my friend his retirement. He earned it after working thirty years for the Department of Corrections. I was a little jealous. I wish it were me.

What is that phrase? Be careful what you ask for because you just might get it! Simultaneously during that time, the Department was experiencing an attrition problem. Large numbers of staff who had joined the Department in the 1980s and early 1990s were rapidly reaching retirement age and retiring en masse. The Department didn't have enough staff to promote quickly enough.

One solution was to move me up to the next classification in an acting capacity. That greatly benefited the Department, more than it benefited me, as I received all the responsibilities of that classification without the pay raise. Respectfully declining was not an option and was severely frowned upon. For the foreseeable future, I was the acting Associate Warden of Healthcare. I was tasked with the DNA and TB operations while continuing to ensure the HCA mission continued without an HCA Captain. I had three years to retire.

My health began to decline much more rapidly. Twice during that year, I thought I was having a heart attack. Twice I left the Institution in an ambulance.

The first time I was sitting in my office in the Correctional Treatment Center with the door closed. The right side of my body went numb and began to tingle. I sat there unable to catch my breath, sweating and trembling. Living in a constant state of code yellow and/or fight or flight was wreaking havoc on my body. A constant rush of cortisol can confuse your immune system and lead to physical exhaustion. I tried to remember the symptoms of a heart attack in women, and how the symptoms presented differently than in men. I had to talk myself into opening my office door and asking for help. I sat in the Institution's medical facility, surrounded by medical staff and I had to force myself to ask for help when I thought I might be dying. Why? I didn't want anyone to know that I was struggling, and had been for quite a while. In the prison environment, weakness is not tolerated. By staying silent, was I going to sit there and allow myself to die? No, I wasn't. I opened my office door. I quietly told the Chief Registered Nurse what was happening. Of course, everything I was trying to avoid happened. She sounded the alarm, as she was required to do. The call went out on the institutional radio. An ambulance was summoned and some of my staff, peers, Supervisors, and friends responded to the CTC. I was forced to relinquish control and was whisked away to the local hospital. The diagnosis was low potassium, but I knew what it was. I had a panic attack, as the walls were closing in on me.

I was working at least 60 hours per week. I didn't have time to take care of myself. I wasn't eating right, and I wasn't able to sleep most nights. Instead of taking time off to take care of myself as any rational person would. I pushed myself harder.

When both operations were completed, I was invited to be a member of a CCHCS audit team for a week, at the prison in Tehachapi. I was excited to go, as I thought I could use a break from LAC and a change of venue might do me some good. I hoped I could learn new policies and procedures I could apply to my position as HCA Captain at LAC, as well as network to make new contacts at headquarters. I never knew when an opportunity might fall in my lap and as the saying goes, if I stayed ready, I wouldn't have to get ready.

The California Correctional Institution (CCI) was originally opened in 1933, housing incarcerated women. In July 1952, an earthquake closed the facility. In 1954, CCI reopened as a male Institution. In 1985 and 1986, the state built two new maximum-security facilities that were considered state-of-the-art at the time.

The following year the prison added a new high-medium custody facility. The prison is located approximately sixty miles north of LAC. The one-hour drive is through the treacherous Tehachapi Mountains. I was expected to drive to the Institution every day for a week.

When I arrived on the first day, I was the only woman and only Black person on a team of approximately eight Hispanic and White men, including the Director of CCHCS. It wasn't usual. I often found myself as the only woman and the only Black person in many spaces throughout my life, as well as my career. The Director was very warm and welcoming, but he didn't have any expectations of me for the week. I was a token. I felt like the mascot of the audit team. I was confused and disappointed and wasn't sure if that was the norm, or if I was being set up to fail. If I failed I am sure it would be reported to my Warden at LAC, as well as to headquarters. To add insult to injury, they did not assign me a laptop like everyone else on the team!

The lack of expectations did not work for me. I needed to know what was expected. I was required to take that treacherous drive through those mountains every day and since I didn't know anyone at CCI, I had no clue how I was expected to fill my time. When I told the Director, he reluctantly gave me an assignment that required me to work directly for him, but he still did not assign me a computer. Luckily, we were assigned to a decommissioned area of the Institution. So, I took it upon myself to utilize the secretary's computer located outside the conference room where we were stationed. It was interesting, to say the least. I am sure I looked like their secretary, instead of a member of the audit team. I am glad I stayed, instead of asking to return to LAC because I enjoyed the week with the team. When the audit was complete, I lightheartedly, reminded the Director that as a Black woman, I checked two boxes for diversity. I added value to his, as well as any other team. When I reported back to my Institution, the Director's secretary called and offered me the opportunity to serve on any audit team I chose in the State of California. A few weeks later, I took them up on their offer and worked with them again at an Institution in Northern California. Because I overlooked my apparent tokenism and added value to the team, I received the networking opportunities I hoped for.

After I returned to LAC, I was "offered" a new position. I use the word offered loosely, because I did not have a choice. The CDW explained that the Institution "needed" me as the acting Associate Warden of Facilities C and D. The two worst facilities in the Institution. Those two yards are where the most assaults, Rules Violation Reports, and staff disciplinary actions happened. Of course, there were junior Captains I had much more seniority than, and who could have greatly benefited from the experience. But no, LAC stayed true to form. Always working their workhorses and worker bees to death. Being good at your job often attracts more work. It's called performance punishment. They were over-utilizing their high performing staff, while under-utilizing their low performers. I had intended to stay in HCA until I retired. Why not? I had more than earned my stripes. Yea, that wasn't going to happen. The Warden thought my talents were being "wasted" in HCA. Translation: "Where can we work her to death?" Again, I found myself coming in early and being the last to leave. But this time, I was coming in on my days off. That is also where I earned my second trip from the Institution to the hospital in an ambulance.

The second time it happened, I was again, sitting at my desk. Unbeknownst to me, I had begun moaning while breathing heavily. My chest was hurting, and I was sweating profusely. I closed my eyes and laid my head down on my desk, just hoping to catch my breath. Luckily, my office door was open this time, and my staff heard me struggling. When I opened my eyes and looked up, they were in the doorway staring at me. Before I could say anything, everything was in motion the same as before. A radio call, then an ambulance whisked me away to the hospital. This time for some reason I was embarrassed. Two health emergencies in as many months. It meant something was happening that I could not control. Something needed to change, but I didn't know what. I was at a loss.

When I arrived back at work the next day my mask was firmly back in place. Never let them see you sweat, and never let them make you cry was my mantra for so long that I didn't know how to do anything else. I didn't know what I needed to do, but I knew I needed to do something, or the Department was going to kill me.

Then out of the blue, I was thrown what I thought was a lifeline. I received a call from girlfriend who was the Warden at Chino Institution for Men, in Chino, California. She had been promoted to Warden the year before from LAC. I hadn't seen her in over a year, but we had kept in touch. During our conversation, which I thought was simply two old friends catching up, she told me twice that she had three vacant Captain positions at her Institution. The third time she said it, not only did I hear her, I understood what she was saying. She was offering me a job. A transfer from LAC. When I realized it was a job offer, the questions began rushing to me. Could I really transfer? Could I start over? Did I want to leave the Institution where I worked my entire career? Was that part of the plan? What would I do with my house? I know I didn't want to commute, as Chino was 60 miles to the South East. I would be trading one set of problems for another.

My plan had always been to live in Lancaster and work at LAC until I retired. Then I would sell everything and relocate to Houston, Texas, where my daughter, my only child lived with her family. I missed her so much, and the loneliness had only added to my stress. I was usually methodical in my plans. I did not do well thinking outside the box and making decisions on the fly, but I was dying inside, and this felt like a lifeline. My salvation.

I decided to transfer to Chino hoping that whatever ailed me at LAC did not transfer with me. The next several months were a haze of activity. I decided that commuting was out of the question. It was not an option. I would have to move, which meant looking for a house. Luckily, a good realtor was recommended that ultimately found me my new home.

The transfer package was a horse of a different color. It was an unnecessarily long process, as most things in CDCR are. I was required to get the signatures of all departmental heads, to ensure I would not take anything with me that belonged to the Institution. I decided to walk the package through myself as it wasn't unusual for a transfer package to sit trapped on a manager's desk for weeks. I didn't have that kind of time. I hired a moving company, packed my belongings, and got the hell out of dodge. It took me two months from start to finish. The Warden offered me anything I wanted to stay. I respectfully declined. I got out of there so fast you would have thought the devil himself was after me. In my state of mind, you would have had a hard time convincing me otherwise.

Deuces LAC, I'll see you on the flip side! A brand-new start was just what I needed.

CALIFORNIA INSTITUTION FOR MEN (CIM)

CHAPTER 19

CALIFORNIA INSTITUTION FOR MEN (CIM)

The California Institution for Men (CIM) is a male-only state prison located in the city of Chino, San Bernardino County, California. It is often called "Chino." CIM opened in 1941 and was the first major minimum-security prison built and operated in the United States. It was only the fourth prison built in the State of California. Over the years, there were many movies and documentaries made about it. It was famous for a few things, but infamous for many more.

Inmate Kevin Cooper escaped from CIM in 1983. Three days after his escape, four people were found dead in nearby Chino Hills. Cooper was later convicted of the murders.

Shayne Allyn Ziska was a Correctional Officer at CIM from January 1984 through October 2000. In 2004, he was arrested for helping the Nazi Lowriders (a white supremacist prison gang) distribute drugs and assault inmates inside CIM. He was convicted on charges of conspiracy, civil rights violations, and violent crime in aid of racketeering.

Correctional Officer Manuel Gonzalez Jr. was stabbed to death in 2005. Officer Gonzalez began his career at CSP-LAC before transferring to Chino. Factors that may have contributed to the killing were prison overcrowding, understaffing, and a failure to segregate the inmate in question due to a history of violent behavior, the inmate's lengthy stay at CIM, the inmate's access to a weapon, and the Officer's lack of a protective vest.

On August 8, 2009, a prison riot broke out at CIM during which over two hundred and fifty inmates were injured, and 50 inmates were taken to nearby hospitals. It ultimately took more than twelve hours to put down. The riot was mainly between Hispanic and Black inmates. The prison was severely damaged. The riot caused a lockdown of the prison and six other prisons in the area for more than six months.

It is not uncommon when someone promoted up the chain of command at a different Institution to take a team with them. If you are willing to transfer, you can find a place at the new Institution. It made sense for a multitude of reasons; they could surround themselves with familiar people they trusted. They already knew their team's work ethic and knew they would work hard for them. Also, they needed people who would have their back in an unfamiliar environment.

However, what could be problematic with such practices, I would later find out, is often the staff at the new Institution has animosity towards you. Which could make them more difficult to manage and almost impossible to make friends with.

In my first week at Chino, I ran into a comrade I hadn't seen in at least fifteen years. The last time I saw her we were both Officers at LAC. I was genuinely excited to see her. She was a familiar face. When we saw each other, we hugged and spent a few minutes catching up on the last 15 years. The next thing she said stunned me.

"What made you do that?"

"Do what?" I answered as I didn't know what she was referring to.

"Become a Captain?"

I was so confused that I repeated the question.

"Why did I become a Captain?" Oh, then it hit me. It was a put-down. I should have recognized it by the way she screwed up her face when she asked the question. Well, so much for rekindling a friendship.

"Because I wanted to promote and earn as much as I can before I retire." I was a little pissed off at that point. "But more than anything, I wanted a seat at the table."

It was her turn to look confused.

"You know, the table where all the decisions are made, where the policies are written."

I know she was left confused and didn't get it, as most people didn't.

Not a great start to my new life. If I could not rekindle friendships with people I had known all those years ago, what chance did I have to make new ones?

We said our goodbyes and went our separate ways. I thought about that exchange for most of that day. To be clear, there is absolutely nothing wrong with being a lifelong Correctional Officer, but if you desire to move up, surround yourself with those who have already done so. Those who can mentor you. Those who can motivate you. Those people who can show you how to get where they are. Your circle is very important. They will either pull you up or pull you down.

We were not the only LAC alums at Chino. Chino was sometimes called LAC East because so many staff had transferred there over the years. The Chief Deputy Warden had transferred there a decade before me and had quickly risen through the ranks. There was an Associate Warden, a Lieutenant, and any number of Correctional Officers that I had previously worked with at LAC that were already at Chino when I arrived. They called us the "LAC gang." I'm not sure if it was said affectionately or not, but that's what they called us.

I transferred with high hopes. Girlfriend was my Warden again, and everything should have been wonderful. I had already worked for her many times throughout my career so this should not have been any different. In theory, my last two years should have been a cakewalk. They should have been my easiest. My career was on the decline, and I was almost at the end. I was a Captain with one of the highest seniorities when I arrived. I should have been able to write my own ticket. Rest on my laurels. Unfortunately, that was not the case.

She worked me like a mule. I was very disappointed. I didn't like it one bit, but I understood it. Girlfriend and I had known each other for over thirty years by the time I transferred to Chino. We had been through good and bad times together. Often working side by side to get the job done. Back in the day, when I was the Second Watch, Watch Commander one of my main responsibilities was to hire staff, to ensure the Institution was appropriately covered per the guidelines. That wasn't always easy, because from Halloween to the MLK holiday, sick calls would skyrocket. If Officers were not successful in obtaining a holiday at least thirty days in advance, they were shit out of luck. Even when the Department began requiring a doctor's note to return to work, it did little to stem the tide. Most weekends during the holiday season, we didn't have enough Officers or Supervisors. I was always more disappointed in the Sergeants and Lieutenants.

They were supposed to lead by example, but they rarely did. Due to a lack of staff, unfortunately, on those days, I was forced to run the Institution on a modified, First Watch program. The inmates could walk to chow but would be locked up for the remainder of the day. It was the only way to maintain the safety and security of the Institution for both staff, and inmates.

On several occasions, when I would call girlfriend to vent about my dilemma, she would come in and help me cover the Institution. She didn't have to. It was my responsibility, not hers, but she did. What would be considered highly unusual anywhere else became the norm at LAC. On any given holiday you could find me, the Chief Deputy Warden, and an Acting Lieutenant covering the entire Institution. Interestingly enough, although stressful at the time, those are some of my fondest memories of working for girlfriend.

I understood that the issues I faced at the Captain's level, paled in comparison to what happened to her as a Black woman at the Chief Deputy Warden and Warden's level. The pressure she was under was tremendous. So, although I was disappointed, I set about helping her run the Institution and dragging it into the 21st century kicking and screaming.

Chino was so old; its policies and procedures were as antiquated and outdated as the Institution itself. There were CDCR forms they did not have and had never heard of. The Institution was like a grumpy old man who didn't want to learn anything new. Of course, we became persona non grata to our subordinates, peers, and managers. Not a chance in hell at making new friends. It would be a long two years! As usual, I put my head down and went into overdrive while the phrase "out of the frying pan into the fire" played on repeat in my head.

As the Captain with one of the highest seniority, I should have received a cushy job. There were plenty available. Chino wasn't even a Level IV Institution. It consisted of a Minimum Yard, a Level II and III yard, along with a Triage Treatment Area, and Administration Segregation. Of course, that would be too much like right. It would be fair. It didn't happen. Once again, I got the worst assignments. The highest security level yard, Custody Captain, and Administrative Segregation, while Captains with less seniority got HCA, Minimum yard, and Level II assignments.

I was always the mule; always the clean-up woman. Cleaning up a program or disciplining staff. I was also acting Associate Warden for half the time I was there. All the work and none of the glory again. I was becoming disgruntled and had a sneaking suspicion I was brought there for other reasons.

THE CCII

It turns out that girlfriend had an ulterior motive. She was having problems with a particular CCII on the Level III yard. She assigned me to that facility to handle it, or should I say, to handle her. The CCII in question was also a transfer from LAC. We had history, and not a good one.

CCII Ava was short in stature, but big in attitude. People often used words like sassy and spunky to describe her. I didn't like her because she was mean. She had a thick accent which made it hard to understand her and she would become frustrated and would scream at you in Spanish. Who does that in a professional environment, and why was it allowed? My last encounter with her had been many years ago at LAC before she transferred to Chino. I dealt with Ava when LAC had a mission change and became a Reception Center, and all the Counselors were moved to education, into a community space we shared. We fell out several times because she rudely played her music loud enough for all of us to hear, instead of using headphones like everyone else. When I asked her to turn her music down, she called me a racist. Apparently, to her, I was racist because I wanted her to turn down her Spanish music. I didn't stand for that! I filed several complaints about her. We all received "sensitivity training" and lessons on how to work together as a team. Instead of dealing with her directly, as was par for the course. From then on, I hated her, and she hated me. My first task at Chino was supervising her. I thought it was a recipe for disaster.

You know the phrase, "The best defense, is a good offense?" It is a principle of war. When Ava heard through the grapevine that I was transferring to Chino as a Captain, she began to tarnish my good name. Several Counselors later told me that before I arrived, she told everyone that I was a racist and I didn't like her because she was Hispanic. That told me just what I was up against.

When I was assigned as her supervisor, I conducted a thorough investigation and found out what I was dealing with. She was a holy terror and not one manager had documented any previous incidents of insubordination. As per usual, her previous supervisors and managers had passed her along instead of dealing directly with her. Once again doing everything in their power to avoid being the "bad guy." They did not want to be involved in the inevitable complaints and appeals she would surely file. In essence, they let their subordinate bully them. I wasn't the one and she would soon find out. She should have never been a supervisor. Anyway, she was my problem now.

The tactic of many lazy employees is to file complaints. Complain of reverse discrimination, workplace harassment, being singled out, and having to work in a hostile work environment, instead of just doing the job they are paid to do. Isn't it just easier to do your job? Apparently not. She filed several Equal Employment Opportunity (EEO) complaints against me citing racism because she was Hispanic.

That dance went on for a year. She would fail to report to her office. I would locate her and give her a direct order to report to the facility. She would fail to report to her office and leave the Institution citing a hostile work environment or workplace discrimination. Meanwhile, Level III inmates languished in Administrative Segregation and the CCIs she supervised went untrained. When she failed to show up, I had to bump someone up to her position to do her job in her absence or do her job myself.

All the while, I methodically documented all occurrences, and all direct orders she failed to follow. I documented the inmates who languished in Administrative Segregation due to her inability to do her required duties. I provided training, then a verbal warning, and several letters of instructions followed. I attempted to have her sign her post orders. She refused. I gave training to all the Counselors and had them sign their post orders, to avoid singling her out. It continued along those lines until I had enough documented evidence to submit for administrative review to my direct supervisor.

My direct supervisor was an Associate Warden who was also a LAC alum. He had previously worked with us, and transferred to Chino after me. He sustained the action I recommended, which was termination and separation from the state.

Unbeknownst to me, a week before I submitted my package there was an incident between the CCII and the Warden. The CCII was hostile. After a meeting with the Warden, to once again complain about me and workplace harassment, she refused to leave the Warden's office upon the conclusion of the meeting. She didn't leave until she was threatened to be forcibly removed and escorted out of the Institution. When the Warden received my administrative review package, she added her memorandum, and forwarded it to Sacramento for disposition.

Once that was completed, I finally received a job change. I worked in a lot of different positions. I had a short stop on the Level II yard. I was assigned to Administrative Segregation longer than I should have been. I was the Custody Captain for some time, and that's where I was assigned when the hunger strike began.

HUNGER STRIKE

A hunger strike is a method of non-violent resistance or pressure in which inmates refuse meals and/or fluids for religious, political, mental health, or other grievance-related reasons, usually to achieve a specific goal.

The inmates at Pelican Bay State Prison began a hunger strike, and it was filtering down to all the other Institutions. Pelican Bay is where the OG shot-callers are housed. They are the inmates who have been incarcerated for decades, and they still "call the shots" in the state prison system. I began my shift that day without any inmates on hunger strike, but the number steadily increased throughout the day until almost 100 inmates were participating.

Inmates were participating in the hunger strike from all over the Institution. The hunger strike began as most do in the prison system. Typically inmates received direction from the OG shot callers, or there were legitimate issues with one or more areas of the Institution. Some of the main reasons for hunger strikes are prison conditions such as food, or procedural issues, such as lack of visits.

Inmates may want to achieve a policy change or bring attention to a certain cause like solitary confinement. My supervisor and I were responsible for the operation. All the participants were identified, taken to unit classification committee, and given a medical and mental health assessment. They were monitored and received treatment if necessary. They were also interviewed and transferred to a central location. The required documentation is completed by medical staff, supervisors, and counselors. The policy and procedure for hunger strikes clearly articulate the roles of healthcare and custody staff to provide inmates with the necessary care.

The Department of Corrections and Rehabilitation has an operational procedure that must be followed. It is straightforward and requires a massively coordinated effort involving custody, medical, and mental health, as well as required documentation at every level.

The Institution is locked down and all movement is modified. The inmates are cell-fed, and yard, as well as all usual institutional activities, are suspended. A hunger strike affects the entire Institution. If it is protracted it can cause major problems with the inmate population as their daily activities are greatly curtailed. The only inmate movement is usually medical, dental, and inmates who work in the kitchen and other industries. The Institution has to continue to run as efficiently as possible during the hunger strike.

There is a daily statewide conference call involving every Institution including the Director of Corrections. It meant long days. To assure everything was correctly done and completed before the conference call, I came in early each morning. It would be a disaster if it was our turn to give our report during the conference call and I did not know absolutely everything that was going on in our Institution. It would make the Warden, as well as the entire Institution, look bad. The hunger strike lasted through a good portion of the summer, with fewer and fewer participants as time passed. You have to be dedicated to your cause to starve yourself to death, and most inmates are not dedicated to anything, much less a philosophical cause. Eventually, due to the media and family pressures, the inmates' grievances at Pelican Bay were met, and the hunger strike ended.

Once Operation Hunger Strike was over, I was required to produce an after-action report, which is expected after every major operation. It was important to identify our strengths as well as our weaknesses. To ensure the next time a hunger strike occurred, staff would be properly trained and prepared. There would certainly be a next time.

The Institution easily slid back into business as usual. I remained in my position as Custody Captain until the end of the year.

At the end of summer, that year girlfriend decided to retire. I was happy for her. I was grateful for everything she had done for me professionally but working for her was killing me. She worked me way too hard. I welcomed her happy news. To show my gratitude and wish her well in her next phase of life, I planned her retirement party.

Her retirement party was held in the institutional courtyard under a large tent in the warmth of the late summer sun. She looked so happy. I couldn't help but envy her. I was glad to see her move into her next chapter after such a long and illustrious career. I was sure it would be a wonderful new time of life for her, and I couldn't wait to follow. I had one year to go.

CHAPTER 20

THE LAST WARDEN

Chino's next Warden and the last I would work for arrived quietly without much fanfare. I was ecstatic that the Department chose him for the Institution instead of promoting someone from within. He was an outsider just like me. I would have been miserable trying to dodge someone who may or may not have had a grudge against me for something real or imagined. I didn't go out of my way to find out anything about him in advance; no rumors or institutional scuttlebutt. I was sure he would be just like every other Warden I ever worked for. More interested in what I could do for him and the Institution, than what he could do for me. Of course, that was not entirely true. I worked for some genuinely nice Wardens in my day. To say I was a little bitter and a lot disillusioned by then would be an understatement. Nevertheless, I thought the new Warden and I would get along just fine.

When he arrived, I was still the Custody Captain. We were severely short-staffed and needed to hire Sergeants and Lieutenants immediately. I assembled the team to conduct the interviews and complete the hiring packages. It took several months, but I got the job done. A few months later, for whatever reason, I was transferred to Facility A. It was a Level II, but a facility, nonetheless. I still did not enjoy being a Facility Captain. I never did, but I continued doing my job without any issues. Then I was transferred to Administrative Segregation. Are you kidding me, with my seniority? I had been there before. When there were at least four Captains with less seniority than me, why would I be assigned to Administrative Segregation? It was a rhetorical question. I already knew the answer. It was because I had classification experience from all those years of being a Correctional Counselor. Same story, different day, different Institution.

One of the worst things about Administrative Segregation at Chino is because it is such an old Institution there weren't any windows in my office. It was built in the 1940s when they didn't know how important sunlight is to mental health. I would end my career working in a damp, dark, windowless cave. Whatever was ailing me at LAC, found me at Chino. My dear mother used to say, "You take yourself with you wherever you go." She ain't never lied. It turned out I was the problem. I was my own worst enemy. Always doing too much but demanding too little.

Constantly trying to prove myself when there was nothing left to prove. It was becoming a nightmare. To top it off, I was lonely. I missed everything about LAC. Everything and everyone. I missed the city, and the Institution. Most of all I missed the camaraderie of my tribe. It never occurred to me that I was likely clinically depressed. Having left everything and everyone I knew to transfer to a different Institution in the twilight of my career. If I had identified the problem, I would have gotten help. Instead, I sunk deeper and deeper into my funk and didn't know how to pull myself out of it. It would be a long year.

One morning, I was notified that the Warden wanted to see me. Oh Lord, I thought, what now? I couldn't for the life of me think what he could want, no matter how much I racked my brain trying. I just had to wait to see.

I arrived at his office early and sat patiently outside the door until he arrived and ushered me in. I had my armor and shield firmly in place. Sometimes, I still wore my shades as a form of protection, so he couldn't gauge my reaction to whatever he had to say or see my eyes. As I sat across from his expansive desk, the meeting began.

"First, I would like to thank you," he said. My eyes began welling with tears. A sigh escaped from the back of my throat. Everything was going to be alright. That last year, my emotions simmered just below the surface, always in danger of bubbling over.

"You are such a hard worker, and you've always done such a wonderful job. You have gone where you were needed, and you never complained. But I noticed you've looked tired lately."

Tears began to spill from my eyes and roll under my shades down my cheeks. I didn't dare move to wipe them away.

"I know you're tired, but you're almost at the end."

It was exactly 12 months until my 50th birthday. I had almost made it to retirement.

"You're retiring next year, right?"

I shook my head yes, as I didn't trust my voice not to crack if I spoke.

"You are such an asset to the Department that I don't want you to leave with a bad taste in your mouth. Tell me, where do you want to go? You can have any assignment you want." he said almost casually. My salty tears stung the back of my throat.

Nobody in my entire career had asked me that question. They always assigned me where they wanted me. Where they needed me. They put me in positions where I needed to clean something up or where I needed to discipline someone. Somewhere they needed me to lead an operation or run a difficult program, or implement a new procedure. They sent me someplace no one else wanted to go; someplace that benefited the Institution but rarely benefited me. I took a deep breath to avoid a sob escaping.

"Healthcare, I'd like to go to healthcare." I quietly stated. That's where I would end my career. Thank you, Warden, for seeing me. You saw me struggling and helped me when you didn't have to.

Unfortunately, a few days later I had an industrial accident. I twisted my ankle and was off work for several months. Even in my absence, the Warden kept his promise and assigned me to healthcare. He kept my position open for me until I returned.

When I returned to work, I started the new and final position of my career. Healthcare was run a little differently at Chino. The Healthcare Captain's office was located outside the institutional gates, in what used to be off-grounds staff housing. That program was discontinued years before and the buildings were turned into offices. I was only required to go inside the secure perimeter fence for very specific reasons. Besides the required meetings and hospital inspections, I sat cocooned in my little house, in my office, on the outskirts of the Institution. I didn't even have to drive in anymore. I found a route that took me around the Institution straight to my office.

One day upon my return to work from my injury, I was rushing to my next meeting and encountered the Warden. We greeted each other warmly. As he had become one of my favorite managers, for obvious reasons. As he approached me, he said, "Thanks, Cromwell I appreciate you." I knew without him ever saying her name, exactly why he was thanking me.

"No need to thank me, I said. I was just doing my job."

"That may be true, but you did it when nobody else would." With that exchange, we both continued on our way.

In my absence, the problematic CCII had lost all her grievances and appeals and had quietly retired. The smile on my face radiated through me for the rest of my day.

CHAPTER 21

END OF WATCH (EOW)

Correctional burnout is real. It is a problem for people like me whose identities are closely connected to our careers. I had the classic symptoms. I didn't want to look too closely because then I would have to do something about it. I'm not going to lie, my last year, I was tired. My mind wasn't as sharp and my attitude was poor. Chino did not get my best. It only got what I had left to give. The bare minimum. I was worn out. I didn't enjoy my job. I had not for a very long time. Since years before at LAC, and I didn't want to do it anymore. I could hardly stand one more day in that uniform and those boots. Not one more useless meeting.

Not another unnecessary report. I was clearly in retirement mode. I was mentally drained and could barely summon the energy just to show up. It became harder and harder to force myself to go to work each day. I had to talk myself out of the house each morning.

"Just get in your car, just go to work, it'll be okay." I'd pep talk myself each morning. Fully dressed, walking around my living room. It worked most of the time. Some days I would call in, take my uniform off, and get right back in bed.

I know I didn't have the best attitude during that time. I had lost my zest and it was bleeding all over my life. It felt like the previous years had gone by in the blink of an eye. Why was the last year taking what felt like an eternity?

When I did manage to leave my house and go to work, I would sit in my office and do as little as possible, just trying to run out the clock. I had become what I loathed most when I was a young, eager, go-getter. I had become a dinosaur, a person with almost no enthusiasm, doing as little as possible. I was just like one of those guys who no longer wanted to work, who refused to fill out the housing unit logs. They didn't want to complete any cell searches, and couldn't be bothered to pat inmates down. They would show up for work often looking disheveled, expecting someone else to do all the work.

It was almost over. Almost time to hang up my uniform, to put my boots away. I would most likely throw my boots in the trash can. Maybe then my poor feet could get some relief. It was almost time to watch California in my rearview mirror as it faded into my past. I was killing time, and time was killing me. I began meeting with Human Resources to make sure I had done everything I needed to do in preparation. I didn't want any hiccups. I had already determined my pension and cash out years before; however, being so close to retirement I had gotten a little nervous and needed reassurance that I had not miscalculated anything. I would only get one shot at it and there would be no do-overs.

I had begun planning my escape from CDCR within my first five years in the Department. When I first joined, the defined benefit plan was 2.5 at 55. That meant I would earn 2.5% for every year I worked and could retire at 55 years old. With 24 years of service, my pension would be 60% of my pay. It was a great benefit because Correctional Officers are not eligible for social security. I knew then if I retired from CDCR I would never have to work another day in my life. Of course, back then, I didn't know how beaten down and tired I would be at the end.

In the early 2000s, our new contract lowered our retirement age to 50 and increased our pension to 3.0. We were allowed to purchase up to five years of service credit to add to our retirement calculations. Originally, I would retire at 55 but with the new contract and the buyback program, if I purchased four years' service credit, I could retire at 50 with 25 years of service and my pension would be 75% of my pay. That became my new plan.

My 50th birthday was just over the horizon. The funny thing is, like most women, I was vain about my age. Each decade that passed hit me harder than the one before. I didn't even like the idea of getting old. My 30th and 40th birthdays had me in such a funk, I stayed in my bed for days, but 50! Fifty couldn't come fast enough.

I spent way more time in my office at work with my door closed than ever before. I was in a funk. A general malaise. I was living a life of quiet desperation, just counting down the days. One of the sad things about having transferred to Chino in my last two years is I didn't have any friends at work. If I did, I could have at least spent time "inspecting" their worksite. Oh well, too late for regrets.

I left my office only when I had to. Usually to attend the obligatory, mandatory meeting, or to conduct my required rounds at the institutional hospital. I spent a lot of time touring outside hospitals and medical facilities. Anything to avoid going into the Institution.

The Department was changing, and I was too tired to change with it. I wasn't interested in learning any new policies. I wasn't interested in implementing any new procedures. I wasn't interested in training or even teaching classes, which I used to love.

All those years in the Department had changed me. Everything was black or white, with almost no shades of gray. I had a much more cynical outlook on the world; a jaundiced point of view. I was always waiting for the other shoe to drop. I had experienced so much negativity and had seen so much damage that I no longer believed in the inherent goodness of my fellow man.

I was a shell of the person I was when I joined the Department. I most certainly was no longer as fun at parties, back when I was willing to hold court telling my prison stories. I was less willing to compromise. There is a reason that CDCR has one of the highest divorce and suicide rates. I knew I was harder, less soft, and fuzzy. I had tucked my femininity away so long ago, I wasn't sure if it even existed anymore. I was the embodiment of the "strong, Black woman trope." Taking care of everyone and everything, except myself.

The closer I got to retirement my colleagues would say, "You're not really going to retire, are you? 50 is way too young." I stopped responding to the question. I knew it was rhetorical. They didn't want my answer. They just wanted to see my reaction. Now, the question almost made me laugh. A few years before I transferred to Chino, my favorite Auntie, who knew I was struggling, thought I should simply quit. I was a smart girl. I could do something else. I could get another job, but it was too late for me. By then, I was trapped in my career. I had already worked for the Department for most of my adult life. I was too old to start over somewhere else, at the bottom, and I was too close to retirement to simply walk away. If I could just hold on, I would never have to work again. And after working in prison all those years, that was my goal!

I became more contemplative and philosophical with age. I don't believe we were put on this earth to work until we could no longer enjoy life, to work like mules until we died. I felt sorry for my colleagues who did. Plenty of them worked well past the age when they met the criteria to retire. For the life of me, I couldn't understand why. Their pay was topped out. They couldn't earn any more money. Sometimes they were working just to pay the state tax. If they would retire, they could earn more money at home with their families. Yet, they would continue to show up every day, until they died on the side of the road going home or in a car crash coming to work. Sometimes, they got cancer, or something else would get them before they had the chance to really live. Not me! I was leaving while I was relatively young, and had time to enjoy my life with my family and friends. I was still healthy. "Still clothed in my right mind," as my dear mother would say. Let the church say Amen!

Finally, it felt like the days began to rush by. I could almost see each month fly off the calendar, like a montage you see in movies. I could almost physically see the passage of time. The last year finally gave way to months. I could barely stand it!

At 12 months, Human Resources became my second home. Those poor ladies were gracious, but I am sure they were sick of me. "What now, Cromwell?" they would jokingly say. I would ask one irrelevant question after the other. About something I had seen on television or something that came to me while I should have been sleeping.

At nine months, I began attending retirement seminars all over the southern region of the state. Wherever there was a seminar, I would take time off from work and go. I first began attending those seminars when I was a young Officer seeking retirement information. Now, the closer I got to retirement, I began going in earnest. Taking notes and making sure I had dotted my i's and crossed my t's. I'm glad I did. That is where I found out that because I was moving to Texas, state taxes would not be taken out of my pension. Yay for Texas!

At six months, I began packing my office and turning in anything that belonged to the Institution, except for my keys. I also began paring down my belongings and packing my house in preparation for my big move. I couldn't wait to see my baby girl again.

At three months, I began planning my retirement party. It gave me something positive to focus on. Many of my peers who retired, left quietly. They simply did not show up for work one day. Not me. I wanted to celebrate it all. I made it to the end of my career on my own two feet. I did not lose my job. I was not pushed out. It would be a celebration!

At one month, I decided to leave early, to take some time to decompress before the whirlwind began. I needed to take some time to get my mind right, and maybe find myself again. I spent more time at home alone just contemplating it all. Then finally, the day I had been preparing for my entire career arrived.

I arrived at work bright and early on my final day. I wasn't wearing my uniform. I took great pangs to look as good as I felt. I was wearing a cute dress and cute shoes. My hair was done perfectly. I would stay just long enough to turn in my keys, sign out and say my goodbyes. Two years, and I hadn't made any real friends. It was just a place and people I would happily never see again. I turned in my red employee identification card and picked up my new yellow one, for retirees. I looked at it and smiled.

I asked my Lieutenant to give me a hand taking my boxes to my car.

"Why are you taking all this stuff?"

"Because I'm going to write a book one day."

"I can't wait to read it. Good luck, it was good working with you."

"Thanks, good luck to you too."

I spent the best parts of my life inside those steel gates. I had grown from a girl to a woman on those hot, gritty yards. I found and lost love in that green uniform. I lost both my beloved mother and father. The Department gave me a career and became my family. I was grateful, and just as grateful that it was over.

As I walked through the gate for the last time, I could hear inmates calling cadence in the distance. There was a slight smell of sulfur in the air from the gun range. My eyes welled with tears. A few rolled down my face. Tears of sadness and joy. I looked around, almost dazed. This is what almost 25 years of your life came down to? No bands. No parades. It was bittersweet. It would be the last time I ever stepped foot in prison again. It was the end of my career. The end of this chapter of my life. The end of my watch.

EPILOGUE

PARTY OVER HERE!

My retirement party was a festive affair. It was held at a local, upscale hotel. My family, friends, peers, and colleagues were in attendance. These were the most important people in my life. I wanted to have a celebratory affair for a multitude of reasons; the least of which was I wanted to show my nieces and nephews what could be accomplished by hard work and dedication.

I wanted to celebrate! If I could have had a ticker-tape parade, I would. I would be the Grand Marshall sitting on top of the float, waving at the crowd. A 25-year career is an accomplishment, and a testimony. I spent the majority of the day pampering myself. It had been a long time since I had done something just for me. I had my hair and make-up professionally done along with a fresh manicure and pedicure. If this was my swan song, I would be the belle of the ball! Girlfriend returned the favor and helped me plan the party. She gave me back what I had given her the year before. Even if she hadn't, I was intent on throwing myself the biggest party I had ever had.

As I entered the party that night, I was dressed to the nines. I had picked out my dress weeks in advance. The party was everything I dreamed it would be. There was just a moment, when a wave of sadness engulfed me. Of course, it was a joyous occasion, but it saddened me that my parents did not live to enjoy the celebration. Although they were not there physically, I felt them there in spirit, and I knew they were proud. Thankfully, the sadness did not last long as I looked around at all the people who were there to support me. One of the many Bible verses my dear mother always quoted came to mind, "Weeping may endure for the night, but joy cometh in the morning." That comforted me. I was happy, truly happy for the first time, in a long time.

At the party, I welcomed my family, my colleagues, and my friends. It was a joy to have them join me as I bid farewell to my career. My niece hosted and did a wonderful job. The speeches and well wishes were endearing and heartfelt. My absolute favorite speech was given by my daughter, my sweet baby girl. My A-1 since day one. She was there at the beginning of my career, so it was appropriate for her to be there at the end. She thanked me for being her mother, and for risking my life every day to give her everything. She was grateful, and I was moved. I loved all the pomp and circumstance.

After the speeches were given and the babies kissed, the deejay cranked up the latest hits. It was a party, after all, and we did the electric slide and cupid shuffled the night away!

ACKNOWLEDGMENTS

When I retired in 2015, I was convinced I would write the great American novel after relocating from California to Texas. I knew my story was compelling; because I knew my experiences were interesting and unique. Only a small group of women share my experiences.

At the time, little did I know, it would take me another five years before I could begin writing. It turns out, not only was I physically tired, my soul was tired too. All those years walking, "The Toughest Beat in the State" had taken its toll.

I didn't want to write about prison life. I didn't want to think about it, talk about it, much less re-live it. I still become emotional while reading it. It is difficult to comprehend that I spent most of my adult life doing something incredibly dangerous.

My story remained in my heart and mind deteriorating. The further away I got from my experiences, the more they began to fade. The brain is a wonderful organ; I am convinced it helps you forget traumatic experiences to protect itself, as well as your heart.

Additionally, I kept convincing myself that I could not write. The decades of, "Who do you think you are?" played on a constant loop in my mind. "You are not a writer," I tried to convince myself. "What do you have to say that anyone would want to read?"

Thankfully, there was always a small glimmer of light, with a sliver of hope still shining in the back of my mind. I prayed to the Universe, talked to the Ancestors, and asked my Dear Mother for help and guidance.

The message I received was to write it down, and speak it into existence by telling people about it. Doing that would help bring it to fruition. That was a difficult task. I never like talking about things I want to do, but haven't done yet. If it didn't happen I would be a liar. But I did it anyway. To my chagrin, it didn't work, and I was back at square one.

By then I was disillusioned and thoroughly disappointed in myself. I told my daughter, "I am either going to write this book, or I'm going to shut up about it!" I knew I told her that to manage her expectations so when the book did not materialize, she wouldn't be disappointed.

One night, I was startled awake. Don't ask me how, but something had shifted in my consciousness and I knew how to write my book. Oprah calls it, an "Aha!" moment. As a result, I feel compelled to share my knowledge with others.

A week earlier, I was reading a newsletter from one of my favorite authors, Luvvie Ajayi. She is a firecracker, millennial writer, who is a New York Times best-selling author. Something she said resonated with me. She said, and I will paraphrase, "Your only job is to get what is in your head onto paper. Do not edit, or rewrite it. Do not correct the punctuation or grammar. Just write it down!" It sounds simple, right?

That did the trick. I wrote my first draft. My first draft was not the best thing I have ever written. I have rewritten it many times. It got better with each edit. The book you just read is the final result.

Many people helped me along the way, either in spirit or in deed and I would like to thank them:

My spirit community: The Universe, the Ancestors, my favorite aunt Patricia, and my Dear Mother. Because of you, I am!

My beloved baby girl: You are my progeny and my legacy. The best of me is in you. You have always made me try to be the best person I can be, so I could lead by example, and inspire you to also want to be the best person you can be. It is my sincere honor and privilege to be your mother. I love you to the moon and back.

My little family: Quintin – Thank you for taking care of me when I needed to be taken care of. You are my soft place to fall. You make me happy, and my life is more fulfilling than it would be without you.

Adrian and Amyiah – You have made my life bigger, better, and sweeter in so many ways. Adrian, I am so proud of you, and Amyiah you are my favorite person.

My Tribe: Lisa, Stacey, and Debra. We walked the toughest beat together. You made me a better Officer and person, than I would have been without you. We had some good times behind those gray walls and steel gates. I am so thankful we made it out alive!

To my book team: Willa, Stacie, and Juan: Thank each one of you for the part you played in making my dream a reality. Without you, my book would still be a far-off dream.

To the men and women of LAC and CIM: If I ever met, worked with, supervised, or managed you, I hope you remember me fondly. Stay vigilant. Take care of yourselves and each other. Retire as soon as you can. It gets better, later.

If you purchased and read my book, thank you for your support. I hope you enjoyed my story.

ABOUT THE AUTHOR

T.L. Cromwell is a retired Correctional Captain who worked for the California Department of Corrections and Rehabilitation for 21+ years, walking the "Toughest Beat in the State." Reading, writing, and traveling the world is what she enjoys most. So far, she has traveled to over 25 countries, on five continents. She is a well-read, gifted writer who always knew she wanted to write books. Cromwell retired in 2015, and relocated to Texas to spend time with her beloved daughter and family. She is currently working on her next book, a follow-up to Time Served.

PHOTO GALLERY

THE ACADEMY

Basic Correctional Officer Academy—
at the Richard A. McGee Correctional Training Center

THE ACADEMY

T. L. Cromwell—Graduation/Flag Bearer

LAC

California State Prison—Los Angeles County
California Department of Corrections—Monument

Department of Corrections—California State Prison

LAC

California State Prison—Los Angeles County
Tower 4

LAC

T.L. Cromwell standing at California State Prison—Los Angeles County Monument

Correctional Officers Left: Sergeant L. Williams,
Middle: Lieutenant S. Shabazz, Right: Captain T. L. Cromwell

LAC

T.L. Cromwell's First Watch—Watch Commander's Farewell Cake

CIM

California Institution for Men—State Prison Monument

CIM

California Institution for Men—State Prison Tower

Captain T.L. Cromwell's Healthcare Office

CIM

Captain T.L. Cromwell's Level III Office

Captain T. L. Cromwell

GLOSSARY

Central Control – The centralized area in a prison that monitors and coordinates the safety and security systems and supervises inmate movement. Additionally, Central Control is responsible for all institutional counts and prison equipment.

Concrete Jungle – An urban area, especially perceived as an unpleasant or challenging place to live.

Contraband – Goods that have been imported or exported illegally.

Control Booth – The nerve center of most housing units, pods, and specified areas in prisons and detention centers. It is usually located in an elevated position above the ground level. It is the job of the Officer(s) to monitor inmate movement and to ensure inmates are where they are supposed to be.

Correctional Burnout – A state of emotional, physical, and mental exhaustion often caused by excessive and prolonged stress while working in a correctional setting.

End of Watch – In law enforcement, "end of watch" has two meanings. It commonly refers to the end of a shift (some agencies call shifts, "watches"). It can also refer to the date of an Officer's death if he is killed in the line of duty.

Fishing Lines – Made from torn sheets or string. Used to throw things to inmates in other cells to pass contraband.

Green Light – Permission to assault or kill a person or gang affiliate on site.

Hash Marks – A service stripe is worn on the left sleeve of a law enforcement uniform to indicate three years of service.

Homie Hookup – When a person receives something (like a promotion) due to knowing someone, not necessarily because they deserve it. See: Nepotism

Imposter Syndrome – The condition of feeling anxious and not experiencing success internally, despite being high-performing in external, objective ways.

Level IV 180 design – A facility that utilizes a housing unit comprised of two wings; each wing is partitioned into three self-contained pods. Each pod has a dayroom and Control Booth.

Level IV 270 design – A facility that utilizes housing units comprised of three connected sections and one dayroom. Portions of the first and third sections extend back behind the blind side of the Control Booth.

Lockdown – When every inmate in a unit, on a yard, or in the entire prison is restricted to their cell, without any access to education, recreation, communication with family.

Mandatory Yard – When the shot caller of a gang requires all its members to go to the yard.

Nomenclature – The name and purpose of the parts of firearms both inside and out.

Narc – To "narc someone out" is to snitch.

O.G. – Someone or something that is an original or originator, and especially one that is highly respected or regarded. From the urban slang, "Original Gangster."

Order Over – When staff has completed their designated shift, but are forced to work another consecutive shift.

Performance Punishment – The negative consequences that high performing individuals may face as a result of their exceptional performance.

Pink Ghetto – This is a term used to refer to jobs dominated by women.

Police Your Brass – To clean up your spent round casings when shooting at a range.

Rolled Up – When an inmate is forcibly removed from their cell or dormitory.

Sally port – A small exit point for the passage of troops or staff. The purpose of a sally port is to deter, defend, and delay unwanted entry or exit.

Shank – An inmate-manufactured weapon.

Shot Caller – A shot caller, generally speaking, is the top inmate leader(s) in a prison system.

Sisterhood – An association, society, or community of women linked by a common interest, religion, or trade.

Suited and Booted – In prison, suited and booted means an inmate who is always well-groomed, with his prison-issued clothes and boots well cared for.

The Brotherhood – An association, society, or community of men linked by a common interest, religion, or trade. This word has negative connotations in prison.

Threat Assessment – A fact based, systemic process designed to identify, inquire, assess, and manage potentially dangerous or violent situations.

Time Served – When a judge sentences a defendant to "time served," the sentence is the same as the time the defendant has spent in jail, and the defendant is set free.

BIBLIOGRAPHY

1. www.History.com/war on drugs

2. State Correctional Officers train at Galt, by Paige Lampson, staff writer 10/17/2012.

3. Deuel Vocational Institution. "California Department of Corrections and Rehabilitation. Retrieved on June 6, 2011."

4. State of California Constitution, Article 20, Section 3 Misc. Subjects (required oath of office).

5. California State Prison, Los Angeles County (LAC) (2009) "Mission Statement."

6. Thomas Russell, Wendy. "7 year case against city finally ends." Long Beach Press-Telegram, June 2, 2007.

7. Fox, Sue. "Prison, Lancaster Mend Fences and Build Tranquil Relationship." Los Angeles Times, May 14, 2000.

8. The Breakouts ignite the fears of residents who fought the facilities construction, by Phil Sneiderman, L.A. Times 3/22/1994.

9. Inmate sought after escaping Lancaster Prison – by ABC7.com staff 10/29/2017.

10. Minimum-security inmate who walked away from CSP-LAC apprehended in Mountain View—CDCR news release 11/6/2017.

11. Stoltze, Frank "Lancaster State Prison Offers Glimpse into Overcrowding Problem" KPCC Radio, April 26, 2007.

12. California Department of Corrections and Rehabilitation, Monthly Report of Population as of Midnight September 30, 2007. Archived 10/26/2008, at the Wayback Machine.

13. Wolcott, Denis. First Inmates Arrive at New Prison – Lancaster's 252 acre State Facility to Hold 2,200. Daily News of Los Angeles, February 2, 1993.

14. California Code of Regulations Title 15. Crime Prevention and Corrections, 3406; Committed Relatives and Friends of Employees, updated through 1/1/2014.

15. Violent Crime Control and Law Enforcement Act of 1994.

16. Stanford Law School, three strikes basics.

17. Two Torn Families Show Flipside of 3 Strikes Law, npr.org, 10/28/2009.

18. California Code of Regulation, Title 15, Crime Prevention and Corrections, 3268(6); Non-conventional Force, updated through 1/1/2014.

19. Skarbek, David, 2014. The social order of the underworld: How prison gangs govern the American Penal System.

20. US Census Bureau, 2010 Census, P.L. 94-171, Summary File Data.

21. The Atlantic, How Gangs Took Over Prison, by Graeme Wood.

22. The Stanford Prison Experiment, 8/14/71-8/20/71, www.prisonexp.org.

23. California Department of Corrections and Rehabilitation Adult Institutions, Program and Parole Operations Manual, 33010.25, Nepotism/Fraternization Policy, updated through 1/1/2021.

24. www.cchcs.ca.gov

25. California Correctional Institution, prisoninsight.com.

26. California Institution for Men (CIM) (2009) "Mission Statement." Archived from the original on 8/13/2009.

27. Stockstill, Mason. Criminal Neglect: Years of indifference turned Chino's prison dream into a nightmare. Inland Valley Daily Bulletin (Ontario, CA), 7/23/2006.

28. Leveque, Rod. Guard accused of aiding gang. The Sun (San Bernardino, CA), 7/30/2004.

29. "250 inmates hurt, 55 hospitalized after California prison riot – CNN.com" CNN 8/10/2009.